Words of One, Volume III

Words of One.

Volume III

By Sophia Love

Other Works

The Guardian, 2016

Inclusion, 2017

sī bôrg, 2017

Join me on a Love Quest, 2018

The Imposter, 2019

Words of One. Volume I,II 2020

Visit *www.sophialove.org* for these and more.

Table of Contents

Introduction

You hold the transcription of an ongoing conversation with the being I have come to identify as One. It is written here as it was heard telepathically. These conversations have been going on since 2012. They are shared now due to their current focus; this extraordinary year we navigate together. Use your discernment with them, please. Since you've found your way to these pages, there is more than likely some benefit for you in reading them.

Subsequent conversations will be shared in future Volumes.

With blessings and love,
Sophia
2020.5.31

"Let it be said here that for humanity, all of your history has been written by the controllers; up until now. With these words that changes. Within these volumes is found the truth of who you are. It is one that you have never been told. It is told here now, in fullness."

One
2020.11.6

Foreword

Since this text is the transcription of a conversation, it is crucial to clarify in what ways the text has been interpreted to convey emphasis and voice. There are several of these cues, and they are as follows:

Bold face emphasis is used for extra stress on specific words. These are not my interpretations of what I heard, but highlighted that way as it came through.

Italics indicate my own voice (that is, Sophia). Unless otherwise noted, all regular font face body text is the voice of One.

Footnotes and brackets may also be used during the One's dialogue to clarify contextual confusions.

Chapter 1. August

Words of One

4:24 AM

It is I, Sophia. It is One.

Thank you for coming forward.

You walk now, fully upright and on a straight path, towards some moments that will possibly bring you to your knees.

This will be a state of overwhelm in emotion and does not mean worship in its typical use. It means instead wonder. It means appreciation.

What lies before you, is a sense of completion. Within it, you'll experience every emotion and near to simultaneously. You've no doubt already felt times when you laughed so hard that tears emerged. It is like that. Only tears not only from laughter, but for joy, for appreciation, for approval, for realization of truth, for gratitude, for vision. The word "rapture" has been used for the experience and it is an apt description.

It is like nothing ever felt and it is felt at once.

The direction you follow, the path – it leads there. You take it collectively, all heading in the same direction.
 Now.

I speak hear of humanity. I refer to the race in its entirety. It is a collective end point. The awareness for the fact that it exists and is in your line of sight, is universal. The finish line is obvious and clear.

Not on a conscious level, dear ones, not on a conscious level. There is no map or travel brochure. This is a place you head to and are led to subconsciously.

Better things are coming and you feel this, on some level you know this, now. The anxiety has been quelled a bit or had a moment of anticipation rather than a sense of constant dread.

You are now on the other side of the Lion's Gate. Things look slightly different. It is as if a decision has been made. Indeed, it has.

The choice, made years ago and collectively, is about to play out. The people will carry it out and witness and then recognize that they have done so. It's as if you've stepped onto the track now, in full gear, with one destination.

There is a part of you that knows where you're heading, and feels it.

It is not that you are alone and it's not that your arrival is identical. It is synchronized and together and perfectly orchestrated. Each of you has a part that is individually determined and chosen and timed.

You are now on the field, the playing field, and the race has begun. It is indistinguishable from how you felt a week ago, from where you were a week ago, yet you feel it. The slightest adjustments, indiscernible in 3D, can have, now, a great impact and begin massive shifts for you. These are experienced deeply and then

Words of One

resonate throughout your being.

Things Change rapidly from this point on. Focus on your entire world, dear human. Look beyond the political arena, for that is truly the tail on the dog. Watch for scientific announcements. Pay attention to the weather. When possible, feel into societal reaction, beyond the headlines.

Your inner sense of this now becomes your compass, and it will not steer you wrong. When looked at as guidance, and direction, rather than alarm and inconvenience, it will be seen for what it is. Your whole self, body included, recognizes what is happening long before words announce to you what has occurred.

You proceed physically through this Ascension and are not carrying this body with you, but actively utilizing your entire self – body, mind, emotions and spirit, to accomplish the process.

Oneness implies Unity on every scale – within and without – as above, so below, micro to macro level.

As has been said, there is possible now, a simultaneous view seen from both telescope and microscope. All of this to be experienced ultimately, eventually, relatively quickly.

What sparks an occurrence for one portion of the whole will not be the same stimulus for every other. Think synchronized swim.

You will need to hold on to your individual part, while being conscious and aware of timing of the whole. This happens within and is why moments of reflection, meditation and inner peace and contemplation are vital now. A compass is useless until it is read.

Your body, heart and soul will speak louder to you now than any possible headline.

Think of your own life now as going through a birthing process. It is dramatic, intense and while it occurs, the rest of the world seems inconsequential – the world stops for a moment. Eventually, phone calls and birth announcements are made as you re-enter this constructed reality.

What you are in now can be equated to the birthing process. As you notice various headlines and announcements, it will inform you, in a general sense, of where you are in the process.

It will not tell you what hasn't happened or what you haven't felt. It is a reflective component, the portion of the media, announcing a return to this construct that is your human life on earth in this year of 2020.

This is to say – realize that it is your process that dictates what is announced and reported, not the other way around. It begins with you. Always you. The process is whole. It will serve you and accelerate your part in it to take your focus from these birth announcements, and turn it within, to the birth itself.

Respond to your own guidance, rather than reacting to the birth announcement as if you weren't there.

You were. You are. You become now the focal point.

Prepare for a powerful journey with inner peace and consistent awareness of the process. It is not to be missed.

Words of One

That is all.

Thank you.

Goodbye Sophia, my chosen one.

August 18, 2020

6:30 AM

It is I, Sophia. It is One.

Hello. Thank you. I have some questions today.

Yes. Go ahead then.

They revolve around the one known as Jesus. Will there, in fact and physicality, be a second coming of the Christ? If so, when and where is this to occur? There are reports that Jesus is already here and living in South Africa. Are these true?

Would you answer these questions and also comment on any other prophecies and religious stories that are in fact going to play out here on earth now?

Thank you.

Sophia, as the race moves to its evolution, an ending of many themes and stories occurs. The increase in frequency pulls in these open-ended stories and requires that they be answered. Facts only. All truth revealed.

The being known as the one Jesus is one of the better known of those stories in your current culture. There are misconceptions and untruths even there that will be laid bare and exposed. All answers come out and every answer known before this particular earth cycle ends.

Words of One

What I will not do is comment on specifics in this moment now. Times and locations are malleable and must remain that way for the organic collective to direct it purely.

When the one known as Jesus returns, it will be with a slightly different story than has been widely reported, than was said the first time. The one known as Jesus lives, yes. The one known as Jesus will establish first identity and then impart the message.

The moment for that is on its way.

Remember that the mass collective longing for anything produces the creative landscape. The ending/beginning answers every unanswered question. All is to be known.

Are there other questions?

Not at this time, no. Thank you.

Goodbye, Sophia, my chosen one.

August 19, 2020

5:45 AM

It is I, Sophia. It is One.

Thank you for coming forward.

These next few days and weeks are destined to be fraught with unrest, as your money system begins its tosses and turns before eventually, settling down to rest once more.

That rest will not come for several years. There are necessary changes. There are needed shifts. There are, initially, minor adjustments just to bring your system of commerce and exchange closer to truth. In its current form, it represents debt. It is a placeholder for slavery. It is an instrument, the instrument in fact, that enslaves you. It cannot sustain your awakening.

It will not.

There is no way for it to.

There are efforts in place now to control its demise. These will have the effect of opening the bars on the jail cell, rather than crashing or cutting through them. They open the cell, yet you remain in the building.

It is a bit of a maze to leave the building entirely. Debt controllers, i.e. banks, run everything. They must be dealt with and removed from having such power. There are considerations of stability, equality and a sustained switch to a form more equitable.

Words of One

It is a bit like taking the monopoly money and monopoly property deeds and removing them completely from the Monopoly game.

The game continues, there are players and property and assumed amounts of liberty, wealth and ownership. The players continue to move around the board, and incur "debt" moments. How will these be "paid"? What about the "utilities"? What about the deeds, the properties held by them?

All of these considerations are valid.

Yet I tell you that there is no debt monetary system that survives an Awakening.

The first thing to go will be debt.

As the banks rely on debt-notes to function, and to supply the population with cash – there will be things put in the place of debt-notes, initially. Not forever, but initially.

The goal has been always for sustained wealth and freedom of movement. The path leading there is fraught with U-turns and dead-ends. In other words, you incur a great many false starts.

What can people do to insure continued abundance?

There is not much that has to change. The system will not leave the average man penniless or without means. Quite the opposite.

You are about to meet a moment that attempts to catch-up physically to your worth, your actual worth. It will attempt to meet your value with whatever is chosen as the most tradeable "currency". There will be multiple currencies and all of them viable and all of them utilized to "balance the books" in your favor.

This has never been done and a correction is needed.

It is to happen now. It'll be messy for a while, yet no one is left out in the cold, and your abundance and prosperity are assured.

Is there anything for us to do to prepare or position ourselves well in this transition?

The amount of wealth necessary to guarantee a livable, sustainable and abundant life is staggering. It is all hidden deep within the jail and its being released – as you are.

You will be amply supplied. There is nothing for you to do to ensure safety or continuation. These are provided for you and have been carefully considered.

So, do not be alarmed at the coming changes. You will see that they signal your release and prosperity.
These are very necessary first steps.

That is all.

Thank you.

Goodbye, Sophia, my chosen one, my scribe.

Words of One

August 21, 2020

4:00, 5:00, 6:00 AM

It is I, Sophia. It is One.

Thank you for coming forward.

There are times when, for the good of the whole, parts will be removed or cut away. Sometimes the reason for the removal is not immediately clear, even to the one doing the removing. Yet, on some base level, within the whole, it becomes a necessary removal.

For humanity and for planet Earth, you approach such a time. This is all the detail to be shared here and today. It is such a concept that will help to make sense of things as they occur for you in your immediate future. There will seem to be no reason for the specific location or populace affected. There are reasons and explanations on more than one level.

Why do I keep seeing China?

This is a reference to a geographical area, yes. It will not be named here. There will be more than one time when it will help to remember this. There are reasons for everything.

Okay. Thank you.

In other categories of thought and awareness, there are certain and specific stories that play out. It is true for different sections of the population, for different groups.

The truth of this gives evidence for the mechanism of creation itself. It is your super-power.

You all have it. It comes from the same place. It operates the same way; for every single one of you.

The thing about it is that your individual "flavors" change the way it appears. Your personal "taste" alters what looks to be organized down-to-earth creation or mystical magic, that seemed to come from either prophecy or the ether, and thus carry with it its own meaning and relevance.

The mechanism of creation works like this:

- **Your belief** for something holds the seed.
- **Your intent** for something is the force for manifestation.
- **Your acceptance and allowance** for something holds the place for its appearance in your life.
- **Your expectation** for something is the magic. Often invisible and deeply held as possible, it is your imagination. As humans, **this is your most fertile trait.**
-

All of these aspects surround what shows up in your world, i.e., what is "real" or "true". These aspects apply in the arenas of —

Words of One

Religion
Science
Love
Physical properties and possibilities
Health

Every part of your physical existence owes its reality to creation's laws. What rises to the surface of the consciousness of man, becomes the more obvious examples of this. By this is meant certain "End of Days" prophecies and predictions that were recorded and are thus known. [1]

Global realization and expectation hold within it a force un-paralleled.

You walk now through such a time in your history when prophets and prophecies are spoken of and offered as "proof" of the "end of days".

It has always been true that there were those in the race that could "see" scenarios play out; it was not always clear in what context they did.

Yet, the words and predictions remain, having become then a deeply held, if invisible, belief, and thus the seed for creation itself.

All this is to say that as the race now clearly shifts, these scenarios will play out.

---

[1] Reference here is to biblical and other recorded prophecies.

They, in a certain sense, have to; to satisfy the completion of cycles and laws of manifestation.

All things come to their own satisfactory answer. Nothing is left out.

This entire world is your creation, dear human. You've written the story, told the story to each other for generations and filled it all in with your own colors. It is you. It has always been you.

None of what is to come will be a complete surprise. All of what is to come is your creation.

That is all.

Thank you.

Words of One

August 22, 2020

5:30 AM

It is I, Sophia. It is One.

Thank you for coming forward.

There are things to say.

These things concern the way you will come to experience your days. These will be as if you are constrained. There will be a lockdown. It won't be because of the virus. The bioweapon will not be the cause of this.

This lockdown occurs because of several factors. One is an alien invasion that is not real. They will not invade you. You are not in, nor will you ever be in, any real danger.

Two is that there will be a military presence in the street – a police presence. This will be purported to protect you from aliens, when in fact they are rounding up perpetrators of child and human trafficking.

They are also collecting the victims. There are children everywhere and many thousands of them. There are women as well. There are men. Primarily are the children. This is a massive effort. It will be coordinated. It will be assisted by benevolent ET's. [2] There will be confusion and there will be a bit of chaos.

---

[2] I "got" while transcribing this that these would be human looking ET's.

At the first of this, your media/news anchors will attempt to evoke fear and skew the narrative. As the bizarre is clear, this will be abandoned and truth will emerge.

This is a global effort and reckoning and rescue and capture. It all happens in the near to now future of the earth.

The earth cannot shift while holding its inhabitants in servitude or any sort of capture or pain. All is to be revealed now. All is to be exposed now. All is to be announced now.

All is to be reconciled. You as a race, move from slavery to sovereignty, from mass deception to mass awareness, from prisoners to free.

It will be a mess for a while. It is suggested that you have in your stores, surplus food. It is suggested that you prepare to be isolated again from the streets and the stores and the schools and all gathering places.

You will not, in most cases, oppose this, as the uncertainty runs so high about who is after who.

Mass announcements inform you. These are scheduled to be non-stop and unable to avoid. You will know what is happening. You will know why it is happening. There will be many surprises, yet not all of it will come as a complete shock.

What happens for the race is a clean-up and repair. The damage has been severe. The strength of your faith in all that is good will carry you through this part.

Words of One

Confusion and uncertainty will be what predominates the airwaves and thus your mind. Do not allow these to take hold. Know that the deep hold and oppression of man has to be stopped before the new can emerge. The slavery, in all forms and of every being – has to end.

This is a necessity. It is the only way to move into a fully functioning high frequency society.

You will witness and live through this, although you will not personally be freed or captured. It will impact your daily life.

As the end of 3D Earth for you comes closer, all that cannot be altered will be stopped or removed. The halting of slavery on a mass scale and for an entire race, is a global operation.

It will feel messy and out of control, yet it is very much the opposite.

Realize that the show, the orchestration of your society, will end as those controllers of the narrative are removed. This is the reason for the messy and out of control appearance.

The prior controllers will be no longer working or on the job, and in every case, you have come to depend on that voice for normalcy and continuation. The new voice, which initially comes to you in the way of announcements, will be unfamiliar and what it will report – frightening and shocking. Nothing like the usual narrative.

Many voices will be silenced.

This is scheduled to happen, and to be as brief as possible in its disruption. This is the reason for the suddenness and shock. In order for the successful carrying out of such an operation – surprise is an essential ingredient.

Prepare to be at home for a while. It will be days, not months, when the strict compliance to these mandates is necessary. There may be, as well, a period of no communication. Yet this is uncertain.

That is all.

Words of One

August 23, 2020

Note — this is incomplete as much of it was personal. What is included is everything that applies to the population at large. I was looking for information.

It is I. It is One.

Here is the order of operations.

There is a fight to the finish.

The dark one's operatives are desperate, as their lives are at stake. Some play "roles" because deals have been struck.

There are narratives playing on the airwaves to keep the majority of them placated and still operating — so that they can be caught in the act. And they are being caught in the act.

It is kept quiet because of the large numbers of them to catch.

What is the order?

- There is a constant battle until the overthrow.

- The overthrow happens within mass global arrests and capture and saving of children. The underground pathways and nature of this horror is thus exposed.

- The announcements happen during lockdown.

- The military, as well as dignitaries who are cooperating with them, are explained during the announcements.

- There is an off-world element that assists in the process and assures success.

- Once the children are freed, the money/debt slavery is unlocked and altered.

- At this point the people will be participating in the selection process of leaders, commerce and societal management. Some of you are here to help with that.

Those who manage this portion of your captivity will have been exposed already, due to the trafficking and so new leaders of new systems will emerge.

It will be very confusing.

What is won't be is vicious or angry as the dark energy will be removed at this point.

The process is gradual and overnight. By the USA Election * facts are known and lockdown with nonstop announcements of historical significance have begun. By years end, the dark will have been removed.

By years end, the new day emerges and humanity's choice for peace and prosperity will rule that day.

Words of One

It is always darkest before the dawn, and what you are sensing right now is that darkness. It gradually increases. It is a good thing it does — now you know where your light is necessary.

What about the virus? The med beds? A cure?

What you seek is factual, honest information and there is none; not widespread and not trusted.

You've stopped.

The remainder of this information concerns the Pleiadeans and is not mine to give.

I will say this.

The lethality of this virus is not what you've been told.

The fear around it will not subside however, until true facts are heard and then trusted by the population. All of that after the dark is removed. It is a painful process. Realize this and prepare. Emotionally prepare.

You've stopped.

Will you give approximate dates for these projections?

The rounding up of the criminal traffickers happens and is seen now.

There is clarity as to players by the USA Election [3].

There is disharmony of the citizens as they then work to choose leaders of the light and not of the dark.

By years end, there is a clear choice and although details and players must be worked out. There is a sign of slight relief and an uptrend.

This will not be easy, Sophia.

It will be years before the actual shift completes itself.

Thank you.

---

[3] This is a reference to the conclusion of the USA Election and not to a specific day, as in Election Day.

Words of One

August 25, 2020

5:55 AM

It is I, Sophia. It is One.

There are things to say.

Thank you for coming forward.

This is a trying time. It is as if you have expended your last bit of patience and good will, expecting a concrete answer or positive change, only to discover the new day dawns on the same earth and is covered with the same issues. This is how it appears to your eyes.

Yet, I will tell you here and now that each day that dawns new, brings with it – alteration and progress. The process to your human eyes, is unclear. The progress at the frequency level and from the point of view of the heart, is steady and strong and always reaching closer to what you would label the "finish line".

This can be felt internally. For this perspective to be your own, you'll need to go there via meditation, contemplation and inner peace just as often as you are able.

Your body knows this truth. Your heart speaks this truth. For these knowing's to be amplified, there will need to be room for them, and allowing of them. Once they are good and strong, others will visibly notice and join you.

The refrain on earth that requires no help or amplifier right now is that of pain, division, accusation, corruption or horror. That message has been sent and is consistently heard.

A repetitive calling to it, at this stage, only increases the depth of the division.

Not to say that it should be ignored. Only to say that you do not need to add your voice to it, to promote it or create further awareness.

What that will do at this stage, is deepen the divide.

You are on the upside now and reaching for Unity. Anything that you can do to increase global love and collaboration and peace and compassion will benefit the process. Anything you can do to increase your own feelings of peace and gentle temperament will lead you towards reasoned decisions and calm approaches to this life you are creating.

Strength in you, will attract your fellow man to you, and together you'll build the world you desire.

What you are watching is the world burn up and it is happening in real time. Mind you, this is not the world in actuality that burns up. The world that ends is the constructed world based on ownership, slavery, dominance and control.

It is vital to your happiness that you fully grasp this difference. The world that is ending in front of your eyes is one that needs to depart. What dawns next, does so with love and in a state of freedom.

It will emerge when it's ready, nurtured to birth by your own will

Words of One

and intent and of its own accord in right timing. This is a natural birth and the most successful and authentic kind possible. It will help you through this time to look at it this way. To remember what is happening here and why.

Retain your vision of a better day. Even if all that can be mustered is a personal improvement in a single arena your life – hold on to it and visit it often. This is more than helpful advice on how to feel better, it is the inner workings of creation. It is a method that will work to your advantage and right now.

The reason you're here is to assist, and the way this happens, is with your energetic contribution.

Consciously contribute positive intention, and that is what you will manifest. The truth that you control the world you inhabit becomes more palpable for you with each frequency uptick. All that you can do to improve the odds of happiness, prosperity, peace, freedom and love – will increase the speed in which it arrives.

For make no mistake, it arrives.

It is already real. What you are doing right now is moving into the frequency in which it can become the only part of your life that you feel.

You are changing, shifting, becoming new.

In all aspects, this holds true. Allow this truth to take hold of your heart and its resonance will rapidly take you there. It is from the heart where all truth springs and this is the place to rest your faith and your deepest self. Your heart will guide you through, and pull others along with you.

Allow. Allow. Allow. Allow.

Great things await you. You only need to get there.

That is all.

Thank you.

Goodbye Sophia, my chosen one, my scribe.

Words of One

August 27th, 2020

3:30 AM

It is I, Sophia. It is One.

Hello. Thank you for coming forward.

There are things happening now. Changes to your world and beneath all of your radar and out of sight. These things it will help to be aware of.

What happens now and out of sight is a radical transformation Sophia. It is the source of much of the confusion and tension felt by all of you.

People are acting out of character. People are not sleeping. Some are sleeping in abnormal, for them, patterns. You will not experience "usual" conversations or "typical" interactions because everything around you is not usual or typical.

Your world changes.
It is not the same within.
It is not the same on the surface.
The winds and weather respond.
The earth itself shifts and moves to adjust.
Everything is altered within your bodies as well.

You will feel this as rhythm changes and sense this as tension. Those among you (*who are*) most sensitive and unaware are not sleeping. They seek help in the usual ways and the usual ways do not assist. This is a very unusual response to a once in a lifetime occurrence. Everything will have to adjust, including the way you respond.

I'd like to discuss ways of responding as these changes continue for quite some time and your needs for sleep and optimal health do, as well. This will not subside quickly. It will change and it will help you to adapt to the changes.

Listen to what your body says to you. As you lie there without sleep, ask it. Then listen. Focus on your internal organs, specifically your heart, your brain, your stomach. Give them voice.

You have access now, and the ability to connect to yourself in the way you've most often connected to the world and people within and on it. Listen. Your body speaks. All parts of you speak. It knows how to answer for it too requires nourishment, peace and maintenance.

What you will find as you do is a quick response and then, with a bit of practice, a deeper answer. You will need to listen.

For as you watch your external world erupt and swirl with storms and physical changes, these things also happen for you. You do not see these things – **you feel them.**

As your Ascension moves forward, you do as well, and this is all of you that does so. All of you that moves. All of you that changes.

You require changes in nourishment and habit so that the journey for your body is optimal. These may show up as a myriad of new, and unusual for you, desires and practices. Each day they may change.

Words of One

This is not a time to follow habits. This is a time to concern yourself with things that invoke calm and provide assistance in your days.

These things *(listed below)* may change:

Your need for water.
Your need for food, or desire for food.
Your desire for solitude.
Your awareness of the animals.
Your awareness of the trees and vegetation.
Your voice may deepen a bit or change subtly.
Your hair may change in texture and/or color.
Your feet may change in the way they've supported you, and thus your shoes will not feel the same.
Your height may be altered; typically, you'll become taller.
You may lose or gain weight and/or muscle.
Your desire for sex may change.
Your desire for movement may change.
In some, there will be eye color variation.

None of these will depend on age. All of these have to do with this physical Ascension you proceed through.

You will find yourself day-dreaming more often.

You will find yourself away in thought often, from whatever you are involved in. You, at such moments, are visiting yourself completing a similar task in another timeline/life. All of this happens concurrently with your day to day life.

All of these changes happen in some degree to all of you; to every one of you and every day.

You may not notice them all, yet if you keep always the Ascension in your mind as a possible explanation, you'll begin to pick up on them.

It should ease your anxiety to know that they are normal physical responses to the process you complete. It should ease your anxiety and thus pave the way for easing also the entire process. It is wholistic (*spelling intentional*) and organic and natural and body changing.

None of these changes will be/are detrimental to your overall health, physique/longevity/appearance. You are changing, yes. Some of you will not appear to be that changed, while others of you will radically alter your bodies.

This is a personal Ascension and your deepest felt picture of your most optimal self is what eventually emerges. It is not overnight. It is not something that can be helped by allopathic medicinal procedures. Doctors are not trained to recognize this. Some of the more attuned ones will see what is going on in so many of their patients, that it will inform them of a global issue.

No one escapes this and everyone is in some way altered by this.

What will help you is to remain alert and listening. Your body's voice has raised its volume and is telling you what is going on as well as what it needs.

Words of One

These will be different for all of you. Do not be alarmed if you face times of hunger and times of no appetite, times of deep thirst, times of insomnia, times where all that you want to do is sleep.

Give your body what it asks for in these times, and you'll be happier and feel a sense of calm to whatever degree is possible for you.

You'll feel sensations, and often – chills, twinges, heat, coldness, excitement, tension, even pain – all of these momentary. Note them as they move through you and nod. This is your Ascension.

The more often you acknowledge the reality of it, the easier the process becomes. Your body understands agreement and will favorably respond.

As you watch the earth shift and move and respond – you do also.

As above, so below.

The process has no choice but to complete itself and it will. It will be a calm new day and you will be a new you walking upon it and into it.

Allow. Listen. Your whole world speaks to you now, dear hue-man. It is a beautiful process.

That is all.

Thank you.

August 28, 2020

5:30 AM

It is I, Sophia. It is One.

Thank you for coming forward.

There are subjects of concern to all of you here now on the planet.

There are possibilities. There are probabilities. There are conditions which tend to generate outcomes that can be predicted.

What differs now for you is a sense, a very palpable sense, that all of these are manipulated and intentionally so. This becomes obvious to more and more of you as this year proceeds. It is in this way that the Controllers show their hand.

You have, to various degrees, trusted "authority" here. That is, most of you and until now. With their hand exposed you see what they have and question just what it is they are winning. It looks and feels to be all about something other than the good of the people and even about money.

At this point, it is only about retaining the winning hand, regardless of exposure.

Regardless of cost, they cannot lose. What it is that they are losing is control. Without control there is no ownership. Without ownership they have lost.

Regardless of whether or not humanity knows this, the controllers do. They feel as if something has been stolen from them and that this is something that they rightfully own. They fought for it, and have manipulated it for their own benefit for much longer than any of you have been alive.

Now, today, there is a problem. The brilliance of their plan unravels and there are conditions that threaten its continued smooth enactment.

What happens next can be speculated, based on previous actions and current conditions. It is vital to know that your freedom and Ascension is assured. It will also help you to realize that the Draco cannot and will not see or accept this as a loss. That would not fit their world view. Rather, it will be seen as too problematic to continue and then they will move on.

The Draco will not change being Draco as a result of this Ascension. Their process will not end the same as it does for the human.

It is an individual evolution and what has been discussed between us and as explanation has been the Ascension.

The fact of your evolution remains. It is the evolution of your race that has been discussed here, and not the outcome for every race.

We speak now of probabilities and also possibilities. It is important to grasp the nuances of sovereignty and control and responsibility. None of these extend beyond self. All of these are defined by self.

As an oak tree remains itself throughout its life, so does the human. So do the Draco.

The idea of collaboration and Oneness holds very specific parameters to the race of Draco. It will be expressed and defined within those. It will not change their purpose and ultimate level of participation.

That is not how it works.

Based on conditions tendencies, probabilities, and knowledge of accurate "history", it is seen what is likely here. Remember that all "seeing" is based on these things and not mysterious insight into actuality.

All events are created in the moment of now. Until that moment goes "live" it cannot be seen.

What is most likely as an outcome for the race of the Draco, as it concerns the race of humanity, is that it merely turns its focus elsewhere. This is not a "win" for humanity so much as a change of scenery. In order to "save face", the Draco will depart.

This results directly from the Awakening of humanity.

It will be defined differently by the Draco themselves.

All of this is brought up now to offer insight for you into those humans who have adopted the tendencies and operations of the Draco here on earth.

They have done so for money and power. It is not clear and therefore cannot be predicted how they will come through this. It is quite possible that they could be so altered during the Ascension process that they change motivation and regain their humanity. It is also possible that they don't.

What you have being speculated and rumored about now are not facts. What will tell the story are actions. As truths are exposed, the humans involved now enter into the light of day. You will see them and see clearly, eventually, their level of prior participation. It will not be what they've done until now that defines them, so much as what they do now.

Ascension effects all of humanity yet, it will not do so according to how you see it – it will do so in a process that is individual and defined that way.

It would be an error in your thinking to decide that the Draco must change. It would be yet another form of control – to enforce a definition of performance or outcome on another race to serve your own desires.

That is not the purpose of Ascension.

This planet has been under the control of another race, a "hidden hand". This planet undergoes right now a shift of frequency, an Awakening. The fact that both are occurring here is not a definition of either – it is the condition under which humanity chose to evolve.

What is clear, is that the Awakening results in an end to slavery, trafficking, manipulation and all cruelty.

What is also important to realize is that this Awakening does not guarantee or define the outcome or behavior of any of you.

Behaviors and corruption have grown into ways of life here on earth.

The Ascension of Man does not make them magically disappear. What it does is create and maintain a frequency for life here that cannot sustain such forms of control.[4]

It is up to the individual still to stop them as they are attempted. This is a physical process that will be undone physically.

Although magic and some surprises are components of the process, it all happens on a case by case basis. Once the Draco exit, you will deal with the lessons and methods they've engrained in the race.

The strength of human nature and the force of Oneness, as combined with the new frequency, creates a probable outcome for actions based on love rather than self.

What is said here is that you'll have to get there through physical action and also that not everyone will be on board. Sovereignty means that you each get to choose. Right now, the odds favor a choice for the whole rather than for self. It is why this is such a pivotal time. The odds favor Oneness, and Ascension guarantees it.

Thank you.

---

[4] Hand written note from the margins: "This was felt as a reminder as to the fact that it's a step by step process, and that there is no "Mr. Clean" magic eraser to get rid of the stuff we don't want. We'll have to do that ourselves." Sophia

Words of One

Goodbye Sophia, my chosen one.

August 31, 2020

What follows are parts of a conversation I had with my Higher Self first, and ultimately, with One. It occurred initially at my calling, and after you read it, I will tell you some conclusions. It was profound and shocking personally, and all of it is still rumbling around in my heart.

We'll begin with my Higher Self. It occurred after several long and emotional and uncomfortable conversations with people I love, who know what I do and love me back, yet do not see the world as I do. You'll probably feel the agitation and frustration in the questions. Those emotions have dissipated somewhat, yet not completely.

This may just qualify as a "dark night of the soul" and the recovery from it is not quite complete. It is being shared cautiously here and now, due to the profound information that came through when the conversation completed itself. It is hoped to be of some help to you as well, as we navigate this next part.

"I'd like some answers. I don't know how to recover from the separation I feel from ____."

Why don't you ask specific questions?

Okay. How do I know that these conversations are accurate? Most of it hasn't been validated.

You can trust what you feel in your heart. You will need to look at what your life tells you and then measure it against…

I want proof.

51

Words of One

It comes from you, from inside you – you face and right now – the contrast – 3D to 5D.
Which will you choose?

It's not that simple.

It isn't?

No.

The 3D proof (for the reality of 5D) is not here for any of it. Where are the pods, the off-world help, the help that has been promised? I will no longer propagate lies.

Is that what you honestly believe you are doing?

I don't know? It's in my home now. I want proof. Where is the proof.

You have to find your heart Sophia, and see what it tells you.

*I want proof – that what I've been saying is real, **is actually real.***

Of course, it's real.

"None of it has taken place. My family is suffering. These are the things that for me, and right now, are more "real" than anyone speaking to me telepathically."

(Here were listed some things that are very close to home, and they include a friend in the hospital with the virus, and the fear in her family members, who are close friends, the fear in my children, the deaths of two people from the virus who are relatives of good friends of ours. These were middle-aged people. The

violence and killing so close to our home and also close to the cities where my children live.)

"And there's probably more…

*Why is it suggested to me that I share it and then allow it to **not manifest? Why?***

*This is beginning to feel like a cruel joke. Without proof, it is fantasy and potentially hijacking energy from people. Where is the proof? No more "soon". **Now.***"

It is here, Sophia.

Where?

Here.

If I can't see it and my family and friends can't see it — it's not real.

*I live here and now. This is where the help is needed — **here and now.***

Can you answer that?

No, but perhaps One can.

It is I; it is One.

The proof you seek comes not wrapped in human skin, but other ways, other skin, other locations. It does not travel your traffic pattern or route, actually. Not ever and not now. It must be summoned.

Would you summon it?

This is beyond torturous. It has split the very fabric of my life. It is ripping me apart.

I can, Sophia, and I will. Just not yet.

Then I cannot continue. Your refusal to summon assistance for a dying populace is cruel. If help is available that is. Else, what you've done is create a facade of freedom that never intended to manifest. That is something I will not do. I will not participate in this.

Why have you done this? What is the purpose of you contacting me?

The purpose has always been redemption.

Of who?

Of those who would deceive and operate solely for self.

Who does that???

You make it sound as if this whole thing is orchestrated by you, for a select few — That our pain matters not — That until they turn over and figure it out it...

WAIT. STOP. IS THAT IT?

They are human and this is true.

We will not receive help until they seek redemption?
(I was shaking here, as the gravity of what was said was sinking in and being realized.)

Not all of them, but many and specific of them.

Are you f**** kidding me? They will not admit to their crimes! They will be hung, or worse…**

This is the part where humanity enters.

What. Are. You. Saying.

That the race must stop the activity, yes. But love anyway.

Once that happens, they will stop on their own.

The fear is at an all-time high now, from every angle and all sides. It needs to subside.

It will not subside until there is help given. The violence is worsening and becoming more and more visual.

It approaches chaos.

We are breaking apart.

You will not be permitted to break. You'll see.

Something will occur.

Please. Stop with the forecasting.

Words of One

You will come together and forgiveness will override the fear.

Once that occurs, redemption is sought. And then help comes.

I will stop now. (Meaning: stop the current conversation.)

Yes, Sophia, yes you will.

You remain my chosen one regardless of what you do next.

This was where the conversation ended.

Here's a summary of what came through powerfully…

This is akin to the story of the "The little soul and the sun". It is a book worth owning.

The overwhelming love that is possible, comes from us. It's been and still is imagined (by us) to be from an outside Source. It is not an outside Source that changes the whole thing. It does not come from someone beyond us. It blooms within us. **The ultimate test of Oneness is forgiveness**. *We will not forgive other until we forgive self.*

This experiment was and is a test of love. We will not move forward until we accept all that we have ever been.

And then, love anyway. Love completely. Love perfectly. Love honestly. Full acceptance. Full awareness. Full transparency. Complete acceptance without judgment.

We all chose to do it this way. Those who trigger this self-love explosion, have sacrificed so much to do so. The extreme nature of the crimes we will learn about, will bring us face to face with our own reflection. We have, in other times and lives, been everyone.

We will let go of our polarization only when we feel each other as equal. It is the next step. It is not a summoning that we must orchestrate in order to move us along. It is a loving. In that single act, the transformation happens for us all. That is the singularity.

This comes wrapped in hope that we will all realize the brilliance of our do-it-yourself Ascension. It is an honor to be here with you all.

Sophia

Words of One

Chapter 2. September

Words of One

September 13, 2020

3:30 AM

It is I, Sophia. It is One.

Hello. Thank you for coming forward.

Why did you wake me up?

There are things to say.

Please then, go ahead.

You are not heading into an endless trajectory of conflict and disruption, but **out of one.** Your time on earth, has been fraught with oppression and control. You do not know the possibilities for your life, for human life. You are realizing them now, with this current transformation and shift.

The frequency you occupy is one of possibility. The reduction in power over you by the ones who serve only themselves, now allows you to appreciate, actualize and utilize that frequency. You can utilize it to your own advantage. You can utilize it for the good of the planet. You can utilize it for the good of the race.

You can utilize it for the most positive outcome you can imagine.

For as long as your intentions are motivated by love, they are supported and encouraged in these frequencies. You now occupy an environment that promotes your creation and enhances your manifestations. Be careful. Be intentional. Remain conscious. For the journey is not over, although the end is assured.

It is a bit like cooking or baking. You will have food at the end of your preparations. What that food tastes like, depends on your consciousness and skill during its preparations. It is vital now that you **see the ending you desire.**

Remember your purpose. Its time is now and now and now and now. You are here to hold the light. By doing so, it expands exponentially and spreads. It grows.

This is not a part-time job or a hobby. It is a full-time occupation.

I have some questions.

Go ahead Sophia.

Why are you talking to me? Why did you choose me?

I am not healed or exalted or able to produce the sort of miracles and enlightenment you describe. I barely believe it, not for me. Perhaps there are others. I am just here, apparently unable to successfully leave until my work is done. This does not feel like a possibility for me. Not for me. I don't see how I come from this to a place of freedom. So, why me?

Sophia. You are of pure intent. You imagine yourself flawed and in that imagining lies your struggle and your pain.

All of the conflict is self-inflicted and self-produced. I see you through the lens of truth. I see you as you are. I see you whole and wondrous. You have felt and heard your full potential. Your wings

Words of One

are real. I have sent you nothing but angels and it's true. You are among my most cherished. You.

There are those who choose lives of service and you are one who has. It is in the service you offer that redemption is found. It has helped to heal you, provides a cushion of love into which you've rested and now discovered your next process, the next step you must proceed through. You are the most authentic voice, and in your living of each step, as a human, your words will resonate truth and actualization. They are not platitudes or instructions by an "expert". They are instead reminders of a fellow traveler. They are not spoken unless they are felt and realized.

You chose and were chosen for this work.

You are precisely where you need to be for redemption, forgiveness, maximum love and absolute joy. There is no one else for this work but you. It is choice, mutual and global, this this is so.

How long must we wait then?

*I just read some words from Ra that indicate **30 years!?***

*I did not sign up for this to lead people along, some would say, **strung people along** – for how long? For what purpose?*

How does this stop? What must I do to assist it and to move it forward? When and how?

These questions have not been answered. Not directly.

Remember, "the meek shall inherit the earth". Things are not seen by your 3D eyes. The meek, those of you unknown, yet believing, are holding the light. Your saying "You have anchored the light" is true and you knew when it changed. Now your voice and your readers must hold the anchor through the storm.

It will not be 30 years, and not be years even.

As was said earlier and at another time, something occurs to change the narrative. Hold on and you will be witness to the miraculous. It is not a small following you have but a powerhouse of energy that emanates and is reinforced now by your words and your work.

You are not lesser effective due to numbers. It is the force of your readership that changes and alters, expands and holds the light here.

These things you do will carry on beyond you. They will live long after you have gone and that is as you've seen it.

What you haven't seen is your life now. This is created. Created by you, now, as a human and in this current tumult. Do not assume that you are doing less or not enough that is necessary for success. Do not waver in your purpose or frequency.

When?

Before year's end.

What about the US election?

It is an indicator. Yet only of method of change, not outcome. Either way, the outcome is the same. Either way, there may be violence. This is not to discourage you. It is to inform you. The violence is part of the shift and will remain so.

Even after the next event, it remains a constant. The difference then is that it is seen for what it is — an act of desperation.

When is this next event?

It arrives.

When?

It arrives. It is coming Sophia.

By Christmas? By the Election? Before my family reunion? How far away are we talking about?

We are talking about the Fall season for you and the Spring for the other side of the world.

It arrives before winter then?

Yes.

It is meant to be here before that season's beginning.

What. Am. I. Supposed. To. Do. Until. Then.

Am I supposed to share this date?

The sharing of dates has not proved to be helpful.

Gather your family and comfort them with love and fun. You all need it.

This next event is a game change for the world.

That is all.

Okay. Thank you.

Goodbye Sophia, my chosen one.

Words of One

September 16, 2020

2:00 AM

It is I, Sophia. It is One.

Thank you for coming forward.

What you are facing now is the eye of the storm. It is the fiercest moment in a battle. This time, fought more for a show of strength than for any real hope of winning. For the result has been written and known always. It has been written by Source and co-written by humanity. The result will be one that was earned, instead of handed to you. It is your choice that this be so.

A noble choice this is, and, typical of one that would be chosen by the race. For in your most critical moments, man rises to the occasion. It is your way. This time is one of those moments. You have declared yourselves free, and discovered the inner drive to realize that freedom. It surpasses all others and will see you through this moment.

What I'd like to talk about are methods of participation and ways that will enrich and support you in the coming days. For you will feel mightily challenged and even surrounded in what is **not** supportive. This will be illusory, and knowing where to focus will assist you in seeing what is real.

You have with you and behind you a legion of angels. They support you. They whisper ideas that result in positive, collaborative, constructive choices and ideas of all sizes. These may be prayers, phone calls, posts, articles, speeches, or participation.

There are no small forward movements – each takes you closer to love.

For ultimately your residence is there.

It will be challenging in the coming time to find and amplify these moments and actions of love – but not impossible. You will find such joy in the contrast of them to the destructive force unleashed now and promoted in your media. Even a few moments reprieve from that constant stream will push peace forward many times more so.

This greater impact is due to the contrast. It is, what may be called, their fatal flaw. In the push for control now ongoing, what is utilized is a single tactic. This tactic has been known to be successful here on earth and in fact worked for many years. This tactic is fear.

It does not take into account hope or unification or love or community, which are the more powerful human motivators. It is these you will promote and suggest as antidote, and it is these that will win the day.

You engage now in a war of frequency. The tools are perhaps new to your thinking as tools, yet they are not new to your nature or purpose. It is these that give your lives purpose and purity of intent. They are the sorts of things that make life "worth living" and they are being stripped from your everyday.

By hanging on to them in thought and conversation, by promoting them in posts and with action, you'll see their power to unify you. The drive to connect and unite, to gather and build community, to reinforce and support, is so much more powerful than the force of destruction.

Now this is not to say that violence and destruction are not powerful. You are witnessing quite the opposite. Yet notice what you are not witnessing, because it is not obvious and not being shown to you. It occurs as an energetic force and lives and expands in the current frequency.

It is a positive frequency of love and growth. It is your hidden power and one unrecognized by those attempting control by fear. As was said, this is their fatal flaw.

Do all that you can think of to promote love and freedom and healing and reform. For reform is necessary and what this moment concerns. You "re-form" now your society and system of governance. You come to this moment with intention and are not ill-equipped for the job.

Would you be more specific?

Yes.

What is needed now is calm reason that is non-polarized yet focused. This, my dear humans, those star seeds and light workers and warriors who feel themselves activated now, is your special sauce.

You came for this and the moment has arrived for you to utilize this particular skill. The one of resistance to polarization, with laser-focus on unity. It's what convinced you to join this particular party. The idea that you'd get an opportunity to utilize your skill and live it in physical life. Such a feeling it is for the contrast to be realized and felt viscerally. The joy is exponential.

For you know and came knowing the truth – that destruction is a finite expression as a physical being; that fear constricts and that violence creates only fear. [5]

While in contrast and yielding[6] unending power is love and connection and promotion. All of these lead to growth and expansion.

You have before you now the opportunity to physically manifest a healing. It will be unlike any other previously experienced, due to its scope. It is the healing of your world.

These words are said as reminders to retain hope always and to consistently keep you "eyes on the prize", regardless of how dim and blurry things become. It is a world built on love and from the ground up, and will be like nothing you've ever seen. This is because you are building it together.

Promote love always and there you'll find the freedom you seek. Love asks you to accept all participants and welcome especially

---

[5] A reference to the purpose of life itself, and the contrast of destruction – which hits a brick wall and stops, to love – which expands and grows and is exponentially more powerful as a result. It is love that is life's purpose.

[6] Not being sure of this word as it came through, the definition is given here for "yielding" – an adjective; productive, which is defined as having the quality or power of producing, especially in abundance.

Words of One

those tentative ones, newly arrived and unsure. [7] They will not look or sound like you. You will recognize them by their frequency. The power of Unity is unmatched.

Your new world will be built with this power as its primary energy source. Hang on to all evidence of it. Primarily now you are to trust yourselves. Your intuition will tell you which direction to move. You will see, dear human, you will see.

It is always darkest before the dawn. The dawn comes next and once it begins – light will be all that you see.

That is all.

Thank you.

Thank you, my chosen one.

---

[7] Millennials, young people.

September 18, 2020

4:00 AM

It is I, Sophia. It is One.

Hello. Thank you for coming forward.

You are right now traveling a superhighway of emotion, fueled by frequency. It means that things are moving fast for you. It means the possibilities, probabilities and scenarios increase in numbers for you as you swirl through them.

Pay attention.

What you have happening and right now is comparable to a really perfect day in which you've found a beautiful fishing spot. There is no place where you can drop your line in which you will **not** be successful. It is not possible.

Your creation is becoming finely honed. With focus and intent, you create.

This is true in every case. Focus and intent needs to be coupled – alone there is not a similar effect. It would be akin to noticing where the most fish are, and going there, and then **not throwing in a line.** Both actions are necessary for the manifestation of fish.

What this means for you, dear human, are two things that I'd like to discuss.

First is that regardless of your age, history, belief system or reason

Words of One

for being here – right now your ability to manifest what you focus on, see as possible (i.e. believe) and in some way move towards (i.e. do something to get) is in its prime.

As a human body is in its prime in its early twenties, through no fault of its own – so is your skill at conscious creation. You are in your prime with it.

Second, is that this is not magic. You are in a physical realm and belief and focus are not the only components of creation here. Physical action is necessary. Any sort of physical action taken, with the express aim at whatever you are focused on, has the highest probability of success right now.

It is an excellent time for you to practice and to thus sharpen your skill. Pay attention and write down your results. This will help to reinforce what is happening and create further belief and skill at precise results.

This is a fun time for you! It does not mean that whatever you think about and contemplate will manifest, such as the violence and dark actions taken by the controlling element here. What is necessary, the magic wand here, is your intent.

Your belief and focus are crucial components. Yet without action and intended direction they are fruitless. Here are a few examples for you to consider.

Why am I struggling?

I seem to hear conflicting and numerous things. What is going on?

Your mind fights this.

I will center. Hold please.

Okay.

There is the creation of your day. This is accomplished with belief regarding what sort of day is possible. It is not defined so much by the activities during your day as instead your intent for the results of those activities.

You can decide for yourself to be a positive force for someone. You can decide for your day to include joy or evidence of prosperity or feelings of love or evidence of healing or circumstances of compassion. Your decision will make it so. Then, just have your day.

There is the creation of your body. You can decide, before moving into your day or any specific activity, that you see a specific outcome for it. Then move with the intention for that outcome in the way of activity and health practices. When ideas or opportunities show up that are new for you – consider these against what outcome you want for your body. "Weigh in" and see if these promote or detract from your ideal body imagery.

All of these take repetition. All of these will improve with practice.

The beauty and possibility of this moment for you now is that the environment and frequency is so supportive of your effort. You'll have instant results.

As you pay attention to what's manifesting around you – you'll see more and more how all of it is the result of you. This life you live is made manifest by **you.** Your intent, belief, and action or movement brings it to you.

This has always been so. Yet, the static and noise and images from the "society-building-controllers" sort of drowned out this truth for you.

Not so now. Not to the same extent.

The controllers are indeed busy, yet it is a local and pointed effort towards convincing a sleeping populace to remain asleep while believing hollow rhetoric. You are no longer mesmerized.

Allow your mind to wander into greener pastures. Allow these images to plant the seeds for the world you wish to occupy. You are cushioned right now on a cloud of "yes".

Thinking about a strong body?

"Yes".

Thinking about laughter and happiness?

"Yes".

Thinking about a business venture that succeeds?

"Yes".

Thinking about more demonstrable love?

"Yes".

You have numerous repetitive creative thoughts constantly. Choose the ones to make manifest with some physical action. Then, let it go.

Immerse yourself in your life with the express purpose of happiness. Laughter is the greatest equalizer and an excellent tool to regain focus.

You are supported now in the creative expression of 3D/4D/5D life. It is more than that even, the energetic now actually encourages instant creation.

It is why there are daily news items that rivet you and grab your attention.

Use these frequencies intentionally and you'll see your own details in your personal life follow quickly.

Remember that it works all ways, and with every focused thought and movement. [8]

So that deciding you're going to have a terrible day and then telling people about why this is so, will create the experience for you – and quickly. Also, deciding you're going to be swimming in opportunity

---

[8] Written in the margins – "You don't need to encourage creation right now; you only need to create it. Just open the blinds each morning and see the world you want. The pictures I kept seeing were of lousy creations, all that I was seeing was the manifestation of negative thoughts. We are surrounded with fish; we only need to cast the line in!"

for happiness or financial or relationship success will point you in those directions near instantly.

It is a very special time and you are urged to pay attention to all who enter and exit your days. Remind yourself of your focus and intent for each day, as you contemplate what plays out around you.

For global shifts, the element of linear "time" is lengthened. Yet all of your focus and intended thought will take you there.

Watch.

Your world gets built thought by belief by intent by imagining as a house is built brick by brick, by brick, by brick.

Right now, you have the best tools in perfect lighting with the most talented team of fellow creators.

See the world you want. Believe in the life you desire to experience. Spread your belief and sight to everyone you care for, the others in your life, and your world. Hold onto that belief.

The Ascension supports all that you believe is possible. The Ascension is what promotes your rapid acceleration through the chaos of polarization. It does so with amplified light. **You are the Source of that light.**

The lumens that are visible largely depend on your own self-worth.[9] As you work through the center point and realize your core truth, you'll be aided by inner illumination. The more you are willing to

---

[9] Self Forgiveness.

see and then accept about yourselves — the brighter your light and the more brilliant you shine.

Trust.

Love.

Hang on to the truth of you. It is not that you have value, it is that **you are value**, and as such, immeasurable.

There are no parts better or worse here. There is only light. As more instruments of light turn on, it gets brighter.

You are the Source, the vehicle, the instrument and the product of this Ascension. So many possibilities to play with now, each of them directed by thought and realized with intent.

Have fun, dear human. For it is in joy that you will realize some of the more luscious aspects of this physical life. It is with joy that you chose to participate here, and it is in that energy that you'll manifest your new world.

That is all.

Thank you.

Words of One

September 21, 2020

5:30 AM

It is I, Sophia. It is One.

Hello. Thank you for coming forward.

I am that which you are. I am all that is. I am as such I represent every possibility for this life that is yours.
As such, I have seen every outcome.

There are none of these outcomes that find you unfulfilled. There are none of these outcomes that find you in despair. For this is your awakening and it is glorious.

There is every chance that you find yourself healed. There is every chance that you are immersed in love. There is only the light that you are that becomes the obvious conclusion and all that you see. For this is your Ascension and it is glorious.

You are here now for many reasons and many others. You are here now, primarily, for self. Self **is** every other.

The discovery and revelation of all that self entails, is the initial component of Ascension. It is in this place that you have found yourself.

It is the acceptance, forgiveness and love of all that you find that is the next place where you will find yourself. Here you become the singularity. No possibility or outcome is ignored. No possibility or outcome is denied acceptance. All possibilities and outcomes are seen, felt and ultimately, demonstrably loved. For these alternates are other "you's" and nothing more.

You stand now at the doorway. It leads to what will feel like an abyss of horrors and unimaginable truths.

Full acceptance demands that they be not only imagined, but felt and realized. It will not be simple, dear human, or easy to accept these things as parts of yourself. Yet it will be necessary. The singularity holds every possibility. There-in lies its power.

You proceed now to all thins love. You will see what you are not, and in full consciousness, love. It is the only way. It is the only way. It is the only way.

You will have to take in the idea that these things exist for a reason, that everything done had a purpose and a thought that motivated and incentivized its doing.

You will not walk away from this process unscathed. It is for this reason, this time in which you now find yourself, that only the strongest and most determined of you chose now to participate.

You chose to participate in full awareness of that participation. Your effort is not partial. You are not here merely along for the ride or being carried along by its force.

No.

You are the driving force of this Ascension. You represent the engine and the energy, the product and what is produced, the thought that initiates and the picture that emerges.

Words of One

You are the Ascension in human form.

This is not a small idea or easily distinguished thought. It incorporates all of what you do and each element of who you are. **The answer is you.**

No parts of you get left out or remain untouched by this.

As you tumble thought these emotions and parts of yourself, you find yourself confronted again and again with the question:

"Do you love me?"

The only answer, for one such as you, is yes.

It will be personally determined – how to deal with those parts deemed unacceptable. You will deal with them all.

You see now where ignoring them gets you – it gets to a place where they still exist and are found stacked up. These piles of parts are things unseen – until now.

The energy that they are has not gone but been hidden. It is exposed now and will be healed.

The force of the healing, the power of your acceptance, will come as a shock and the stimulus for the Ascension.

For energy never disappears but instead moves. It changes form. It re-defines itself and creates or supplies another effort.

What you've hidden from yourself, dear human, is as worthy of love as any other component part. It represents the composite picture of self-hatred. It calls for a healing and asks you now for that healing.

It is not your nemesis, as in enemy. It is your brother. It is your sister. It is you.

What happens now moves at the speed of your intent. Your conscious foreword movement decides the speed with which you proceed. No part undone. Nothing left to wonder about. All that you have ever been, is brought to the surface and splayed out before you for inspection, examination, decision and acceptance.

You will do this as One. It is driven by your individual heart. Your heart. The focal point for it all; the holder of the fuel for this Ascension.

This is where you shine, dear human. It is the place you've put yourself in order to do so.

The brilliance of your light becomes the ultimate statement. What is seen by the world is your light. Not light from an outside source, but emanating from within you.

For the revealing and the accepting of what you've kept in the dark is a massive switch.

It is here where you find yourself. There are no guidebooks, lesson plans, or Master Teachers to outline your next steps. These Masters are you – taking every step according to your own unique level of awareness and acceptance.

Words of One

The potential for immediate activation by an outside Source has not been chosen, dear human. You chose to do this yourself.

Step by step, awareness by awareness, urge by urge. For in the ultimate analysis this journey will be fully realized, comprehended, felt and completed in one place and from one place. It all happens in you.

Realize that your historical references for what was seen were written by those who watched and heard about how it occurred. Therefore, full accuracy is not found in those reporting's. Full accuracy is felt. You experience now every component.[10] You actualize now your own transformation.

You know what to do. There is one destination and with that in your sight, you can't miss. That place you are headed, dear human, is love. You have only the barest inklings of what that word means.

You will see, dear human, you will see.

That is all.

Thank you.

---

[10] The force for this experience is **huge.** This was indicated with a visual and the emotions to go with it – the horror of the crimes committed; the energy is equal in strength to that horror. These crimes are not covered any longer, but instead converted with this energy. It is a power unimagined.

September 22, 2020

4:30 AM

I asked if there was someone wanting to connect.

I do Sophia. It is I. It is Love.

Hello. Thank you for coming forward. I feel someone else here as well today.

Yes. Yes, you do. Another interested party.

Will they be part of the conversation then?

Not at this time. More of an observer. We will see.

Okay.

Let us proceed.

For you are not alone in your journey now. Yet you accomplish it due to your own efforts and intent; a singular process. It happens only to you. It happens as One.

The contrast of meaning here contains the definition of Oneness.

Oneness is not happening by intent. It is what you are. All parts make up the whole. There is no such thing as isolation.

What happens with Ascension is that your vision expands and takes in more of that which you are.

Words of One

It begins to see beyond individual self while not abandoning the individual form held to do so. That is what occurs with the death process; the individual form is abandoned. The individual physical form, that is.

Here, and right now, what it is you are doing is improving your eyesight. What you never knew was real becomes obvious. The size and beauty and purpose of the whole that you are starts to come into view. You do not lose focus or abilities as this occurs, by you gain them. In other words, you do not lose components of what makes up your physical existence.

You will find, dear human, that as your vision improves, you cherish each component part to a more specific degree. The importance of this body, this lifetime, these people you live with, this project you work on. Whether it be for one person or hundreds – all move into sharp focus.

No effort is a waste. No relationship is inconsequential. You find yourself with new eyes and in a constant state of readiness to re-evaluate what stands before you. This happens for every person, place, or thing you encounter. For this life, with its choices and focus, regrets and accomplishments, loves and loathing's, **is your now.**

It is here where your power lies. Not in yesterday. Not in tomorrow. Not in any other incarnation or life or galaxy or form. Here and now is the landscape chosen. Chosen by you in order to experience the full effort and realization of pure love.

It's what happens here. It's what happens now. It's what you are doing and it's where you are doing it.

You will be enthralled and enriched by each discovery on this journey. For you are mesmerizing as you are, and as you play with all of it, realize from where your power emanates. It begins with you here. It begins with you now.

Not some "you" who lived a life elsewhere during some other time. **You. Here. Now.**

The thrills and chills of life on earth, a human in this current time of 2020, are why you came. As such, you'll realize all of what you are, without removing or displacing this life in its current situation. You chose it all. Every component has value. That value comes because you've put it there. You, dear human, you, are the reason this Ascension happens at all.

What all of this points to is perspective. You are learning to see as God does. The Creator, with every particle of life at its command and in its sights, still hears your prayer.

There are no small parts or people.

This life, the one you walk through now and physically, holds worth beyond measure, because of all those you've touched and met and worked with and played with and loved. Every. Single. One.

It is those you've struggled with who whole the greatest impact **for your own development.**

Note that it is not for **their** development that the struggle is significant. It is for your own, regardless how it appears.

For you are but mirrors for each other, and you wear many hats and disguises.

Throughout the Ascension process you'll be pushed and pulled from global issues to local situations to personal struggles. All of these simultaneous and seemingly happening at warp speed with rapid frequency.

This is by intent and how Enlightenment progresses. It is baby steps and they are taken with the speed and force of a rocket ship. The view is astounding at both the macro and the micro level.

You see more and deeper than you ever have. It astounds you. It frightens you. It confuses you.

Allow it to excite you. You are examining the nuances and specifics of multi-dimensional life, all while embodied in one of the more dense and slow-moving forms available. The contrast of this is one of the reasons you came.

You also came for each other. Your deep love and dedication have built up over lifetimes. Yes, love and connection carries through, regardless of current relationship. You came to help each other do this. You'll proceed individually to accomplish Oneness together. The opportunity to do so, once realized by you, was too delicious to pass up. **You had to join!**

You were compelled to do so by an inner yearning, and also by connection. It was this great party you received an invitation to – Earth 2020 – and you found out that virtually all of your friends were going to be there. You couldn't miss it. You signed right up.

As the excitement rears up and your head is pulled in every

direction, remember those with whom you are most familiar. They represent your deepest reasons for participation.

In this process of world alteration, it is self-examination that presents your most significant and powerful power for shifting. It begins with you. It ends with you. You emanate out and become your world. The definition of your existence is self.

All "others" are mirrors. Remember.

The clearest reflection will be seen from the mirror closest to you. Notice. Look carefully. You are not in partnership or living situations by accident.

There are no casual relationships right now, no "just room-mates". Those who share your everyday, those closest to your footsteps now are your most accurate reflections. They show you your "worst" and your "best" parts with a high degree of accuracy. All now, on Earth 2020.

Your world changes as you see it clearly.

Think about a mirror. One that has been sitting in an empty room, collecting dust.

Once discovered and cleaned, it can't help but show you a clear picture of yourself. Once seen, you notice something you may have missed without the mirror. Perhaps you never realized it was even a possibility.

Yet now, you can't help but see it.

Words of One

You have two choices. You can accept or reject it, for you will not **unsee it.** You now know it's there.

Be grateful for your mirrors. They accelerate your clarity of sight. The thing about mirrors is that they are not active. They merely sit there, waiting for you to step in front of – so that you can notice yourself, by looking at them.

The point of this now is to say that all of your life is relevant to this Ascension process. Those unexpected component parts support you in ways you've perhaps not identified. Pay attention, dear human. You are surrounded with only friends and immersed in only love. Those closest to you, your mirrors, remain there so that you can see clearly what it is you're dealing with and look/be your best for the party.

What an event this will be, dear human. You'll be so glad you came; you'll see.

That is all.

September 26, 2020

5:00 AM

It is I. It is One. There are things to say.

Thank you for coming forward.

There is no truth beyond the truth you hold as real.

Fact is always relative and consistent in that it emerges from a single perspective – that of the viewer.

The double-slit experiment shows you real evidence for the idea that until you look at something, it is not real. If you extend that premise beyond what it is your eye "sees" – into what thoughts you hold as potential truths or possibilities – you'll get an even more accurate picture. Combine the double-slit experiment with the story about the Native Americans and their first look at Christopher Columbus' ships.

The two stories together lay out a more accurate description of creation and your reality.

You hold in your thoughts a group of things that you believe are possible. They are the accumulated possibilities you've learned over your lifetime – your society has learned over your lifetime. When something shows up for you to experience, your mind, your thoughts, put it into a category that fits into something you already believe is possible. Then, you decide where it goes and what it means.

Words of One

Things can enter into the moment to help you place it somewhere that makes sense. Here is how that works:

You hear a story that includes images of something beyond the "ordinary", such as oddly shaped lights in the sky. This story includes the conclusions of a scientist who explains the lights as very specific weather anomalies. Immediately for you, one of two things happen. You either,

a. Believe the scientist's description of what these lights are and accept that truth, or
b. Not believe it, but instead feel it is an intentional false description. You then conclude the lights hold a different truth and indicate something else going on in the sky, either man-made or non-man-made, yet artificial nonetheless.

The initial "story" you heard is identical to what others have heard regarding the light in the sky. Your conclusion, belief, truth about them is altered by your own history, however. In this way, two people can look at the same "story" and draw seemingly opposing stories about its validity.

It is the facet of the human mind that is used against you, and has been used to manipulate your reality, for much longer than you understand. All "stories" have associated "explanations". These are used to catalog and explain and even justify daily occurrences and reports.

The media has become a tool of control and a creator of reality for you.

The technology that is not self-driven, "social media", which drives so much of your life now, allows that manipulation of what you see to be custom made and self-defined. Therefore, creating a unique set of "facts" to rely on that define your reality.

In this way, mankind has accelerated the idea of personal truth and individual creation. He just doesn't see it yet. The individual nature of your news feed prevents that.

It is for this reason that mass announcements are the only thing that can alter the current trend. They will stop your individual news feed and plant there instead, a universal one. It will the one story, fed to the mass of humanity more than once, and unaltered. There will be no choosing what agrees with you to then determine what you see next. It will be a constant stream of "news" and you'll have nothing to define it for you.

There will be no "experts" to explain what it is or skew your mind in a specific direction. You'll all hear the same thing at the same time. There will be only one story and you'll all hear it.

What you decide about it will be personal, but the story itself will be universal. If you are alive and, on the planet, when it is told – you'll hear it.

Once the universal story emerges, your world moves decisively into the next step.

Not until then however.

It is important that you begin from the same place. This is a new

Words of One

world you are building. In order to do so with truth, you need the facts about the old world without bias or manipulation. You will then, together, hold a single truth. You will then, as One, know the names of things and the people involved in those things. It will provide for the planet a cleansing. It will offer a new beginning. It will not be a new day begun in innocence; it cannot be. In order for truth in creation and purity of intent, you need facts.

Not all beings involved in your life are fully human. Not all humans involved in your life hold as sacred the "human" values around life and each other. It is in the discovery of this truth that Unity will be found.

As One race you'll build a new world on the shared truth of loving and surviving and overcoming a manipulated existence.

The power in your joint efforts and combined frequency will be exponentially greater than any you've witnessed. This is because you've never stood on the same ground or viewed the same narrative. You've been unable to utilize your full potential. The division is ongoing and real and extends into, close to, every facet of your society.

Once you add holding a single truth to the frequency shift for you – you are looking at the new hue-man.

This is a breath-taking vision of power and purity – absolute love in physical form. It is this shift that awaits you, dear human. You are in for such a treat.

Hold fast to those you love and to what love actually feels like in your body. You will find there, the evidence you seek. You'll see, dear human, you'll see. It will be a self-discovered truth and as such, will help create your new world. In this way, it will still be your personal creation, only skewed with a single element.

That element is love, and that element is the building block of your new world.

You will learn many things. These will give you the confidence you desire to move forward as well as the explanation for prior confusion and division.

You part is necessary for the success of this, and a key element. You will recognize the truth in all of these words by resonance. **This you can trust.** Use it always in the days ahead. It will serve you well.

That is all.

Thank you.

Goodbye, my chosen one.

Words of One

4:30 AM

It is I, Sophia. It is One.

Hello. Thank you for coming forward.

There are things to say.

These things concern your government. These things concern your current way of life. It is going to be altered for a bit. You will be inconvenienced only. It is not a change that needs to trouble you. Rather, it can encourage you to know that things are occurring in a real-world way that guarantees your freedom.

In order to be liberated from the deep state of control under which the planet operates, you will have to be rid of its methods of operation.

These methods include a common practice of human trafficking. The occurrence of this activity is the life-blood of the control system. It will have to be cut off – in every single instance and occurrence and location of it. This is a global operation.

The stories have not been exaggerated. If anything, they have been softened a bit so that they would be believed. The stories are true. It is so prevalent among certain segments of your society as to be commonplace. Many, many, many people are aware of this truth. Even if they've not seen it with their own eyes, they've heard of it.

Among these circles, it is spoken of in such a way that the human element of the trade is removed from their conversation. The humans who are trafficked are thus transformed into assets or items – much more palatable.

The world will need to be shut down in order for this to be accomplished. In the several possible scenarios, this was seen as the safest method and also one that guaranteed the highest success rate.

It is recommended that you stock up on items that you need to live on. Your movement may be restricted or limited for a bit. This will not be weeks, but days. You will have to rely on your local resources and you will be restricted in movement. You will be told the reason at the time it occurs, but you will have no warning by authority ahead of time.

The practice is so prevalent that many will be surprised by the move to arrest traffickers and halt it. These are people in many walks of life – local law enforcement included.

You will be shocked at the enormity of this. It will rock your world and masses of sleeping people will be jolted awake. It is the next things coming on your timeline of Ascension.

When is this coming?

The timing will not be precisely given for this, even here and to you. It is meant to surprise the world.

This time is like no other that has preceded it. You will come up with new words and terms to describe and define what takes place on your world next.

Words of One

Do not fear this, when it is announced. It is not a bad thing. It is a very necessary process that has been planned for a long time. It is part of the cleansing. Many humans gave their lives so that this could happen. You will see.

You next place to be is one of true freedom. This is not a place you've been before. It will take some adjustments to your expectations. You enter soon a different way of life.

That is all.

Thank you.

Goodbye, Sophia, my chosen one.

September 30, 2020

2:00 AM

This was a conversation of personal questions and answers that led to a few more general topics. Here are those responses:

There are several planned events. Accurate dates for these are not leaked, intentionally, to maintain shock value. There may be intentional diversions.

It is important to maintain awareness, open eyes and expectations for announcements and pivotal events. You enter your most critical sections of time. Once complete, nothing will appear as it does today.

What can people do to prepare?

What should people expect?

There are stories of so many different events.

Yes.

People, again, can maintain a clear focus on the energy they desire to take them through this next segment; the energy that assists.

This will be positively skewed and lead more rapidly to desired outcomes. These outcomes are assured. The road to get there, however, is not.

People can expect surprise. Things will change. Change does not

Words of One

have to be fearful but it can cause anxiety when it alters many parts of life at once. This is such a change. All efforts can include intentions of calm, peace, and controlled movement. This will be very helpful.

These next three months are filled with alterations to your world. October is the start.

I have no other questions.

Goodbye then, Sophia. We will speak again soon.

Thank you.

Chapter 3. October

Words of One

October 1, 2020

2:30 AM

It is I, Sophia. It is One.

Hello. Thank you for coming forward.

There are things to say. These things will assist you in the coming days to make sense of what, on the surface, appears non-sensical.

These things concern the players and their parts. For if you are reading these words, by now you know that all of the roles are temporary and all of the parts are chosen. Once day, the production will end and the players will turn in their scripts and their wardrobe and call it a day. What you witness is the grandest illusion of all.

You do not purchase tickets and travel to a theater to see this production. It occurs all around you, simultaneously, with your life. In fact, it is your life, and you are the lead without realizing it. You are also the script writer, having chosen your part specifically.

This is a performance. Its title has many subtitles and these depend on your chosen role. The title is "Ending the world as we know it".

Subtitles include:

"A manifesto for the creation of a slave state"

"How to break free of manipulation and control" or

"Chaos, confusion and the final days".

Which play you are watching depends on your perspective. Your perspective is determined by the role you've chosen to play.

These are mesmerizing parts, and you are each highly skilled actors. You've dived so deeply into your roles as to believe they are you.

Let me say that again.

You've forgotten, in many cases, that these are parts you are playing, in roles that were chosen before the show began. This makes for an excellent and believable performance – even you believe it.

It becomes a convincing plot lie the more often it is repeated and the longer it lasts.

As a reminder, here are some of the roles:

Antagonist – AKA villain, bad guy or girl

Savior – AKA hero, good guy or girl

Warrior – AKA those outspoken and fighting for either villain or savior causes

Peacemaker – AKA those preaching reason and calm at all points in the play

Crowd – AKA those seemingly swept away by any event or action taken by any one of the first four roles

Words of One

These are the parts, not the people. These are the parts, not the people themselves. These are the parts and they are played by the people. Here is the plot, and where you are in it right now. Realize that at every level and each day, you are playing a part. Your part can change, depending on circumstance and who is on stage with you at the time it occurs. You are heroes for each other.

The story goes like this —

There is a planet. It is fought for and won, by a race of beings. These beings assume ownership of the planet and everyone on it.

Through assorted means of manipulation and control, the native population of the planet are bred to live as owned and obedient slaves without awareness of their situation.

Occasional outliers of the population show up; see the truth and shout it. They are silenced.

More of them show up. There are too many of them to silence.

There is an inevitable confrontation — the climax of the performance — when the native population, having grown in awareness and sheer numbers — challenges the owners. It is violent, bloody, dramatic, heart-breaking, exciting and absorbing.

It is this moment where you sit now.

The ordered control of your lives has been replaced by chaos. There is only the appearance of chaos, it is all part of the performance.

Although many have forgotten, it does not change the fact that they are playing roles in a show that has and end and follows a plot line. It's not easy to pick out who is the antagonist or who is the savior. This is because you are all so good at playing your part. Keep in mind that in order for the best production, there must be an element of surprise and wonder. Both of these conditions ask you to convey your part with conviction. You are excellent actors and this is a phenomenal show.

You've agreed to participate now, in no small part due to the fact that you knew the ending and it benefits everyone. It's a play. There appear to be heroes and villains and collateral players, yet in truth you've chosen your part and specifically. It's not as if this is new for you or that you are unfamiliar with your role. You've held them all, at other times and for other productions.

This time, this now moment of Earth 2020, holds thrills and chills unparalleled. You are here for the show, as well as to perform. Tighten your seat belt, but leave your eyes open. That will become more of a challenge as the climax is loud and potentially frightening. You don't want to miss this part.

What makes for a great ending and a satisfactory show is one in which you really "buy in" to each part.
You hate the antagonist and root for the good guy. It is all very believable. You are invested.

The difference with this particular show is that you are not only watching, not only playing a part, but also intending to convince yourself of its validity. So much so that you forget it's an act. Then, and here's the best part, while deep in your forgetful state, you somehow engage a part of yourself that you were unaware you had. It is the part that connects you to every other actor.

This part of the show is unscripted.

There have been no rehearsals. It is, in fact, the most enthralling part of your role and why you took the part. You wanted to see if/prove that you could do it. On your own and authentically.

The moment for that approaches.

You are ready.

It is a show like no other. You are expecting an ending, a "win", a big finish, where there is a clear loser and the winner is glorified.

The winner of this particular show is not a person or even a side — it is creation itself.

The plot holds many surprises as it approaches the ending. Remember, this is Improv. Even the players are unscripted.

An overall theme guides your role and a guarantee. The theme is Oneness. The guarantee is that you'll realize it, in a moment of Singularity. That moment will be the event you seek. It is self-defined and physically actualized.

It is an ending to top all prior endings, and it has not been seen. You are creating it now. This is the part you play, dear human. You are well-suited and perfectly chosen for it. Each of you. All of you.

Remember, dear human, remember. It's time to relax a bit and enjoy the show.

That is all.

Thank you.

Goodbye, my chosen one. [11]

---

[11] This took two hours! There were a lot of visuals and challenges for how to express what was coming in. It is just so big.

What I saw were two endings. One in which there is a typical, satisfactory winner and loser and then, somehow simultaneously another where there is a tremendous light and we are all smiling, clapping each other on the back in pure remembrance of absolute love for it all. It was pure joy.

October 2, 2020

4:15 AM

It is I, Sophia. It is One.

Thank you for coming forward.

There are things to say.

We have moments that occur in "time" and they tend to reach out and impact, or color, many others. Not all occurrences have this effect. When they do, you can be sure that these are intentional and, in most cases, planned moments. They have been orchestrated to alter reality for more than one of you.

Such things include personal events, such as having a child. The reason to bring this up at all is to discuss events that are not personal, but global. In your world there have been many such occurrences. You have been led to believe, by the "story" or explanation of these events, that they just "happen" in the normal course of life, and in this way are typical.

I tell you this is not the case on earth. These 'noteworthy" happenings are orchestrated to drive the population, or certain segments of it, **in a specific direction.** They are meant to create a social story and to become accepted behavior or even, expected behavior.

Such things as "missing children" and the recent George Floyd murder are examples. Both have colored the population and altered the narrative. They have driven movements. They have hidden motives and been used as camouflage for other things.

If the population is looking for a "bad guy" or explanation over here, they will not be noticing the other guy or explanation over there.

This is a technique of manipulation that has been used as far back as your earliest recorded history, to create a story and steer behavior. In this way it is a fact of your existence.

Only so in that your existence has been a controlled one, and not by anyone with your best interests at heart – but by their own. You walk now towards a time that will be unsettling for you. At this time, you will learn of all the lies and manipulation that have driven your society, defined your expectations and colored your beliefs. Then, you will be asked to begin believing in something else. Something so radically different it will seem nonsensical. This will be a life and society built and driven by purely human emotion. It will be one directed by love rather than control.

You have not ever lived in such a world. It will be challenging to discern who to trust and what is fact. You will be relying on a whole new set of skills and using new tools to do so.

Rather than having the media tell you what to believe or to think, you'll need to decide for yourself.

Things will not be spelled out for you, complete with "explanations" and specific "reasons" to fill in the blanks.

Instead, things will happen and you'll determine for yourself what they meant.

Words of One

"Waking up" does not so much imply that you've been intentionally asleep and thus unaware of what was happening around you as you slept.

No.

"Waking up" rather means that you notice what's going on around you in a new way. For you have always been aware – it is just that you've been aware at a certain level. This level was carved out for you and so well defined and colorful that it was all that you could see.

Again, we can bring up the idea of Santa Claus. To the world of child, he is real. All facts and events and explanations support that. Until the child matures a bit and is able to see things differently and apply logic.

Your whole reality now asks you to see things differently. Rather than accepting the colors and directions that have become "normal" and accepted definitions, you are being asked to follow your own direction, preference, discernment, research and **feelings.** You are asked to trust that inner voice, your emotional guidance system.

What is an assist for you now is that there is a simultaneous strengthening of your ability to do so. This is the real heart of "waking up".

It looks like this:

The world you reside in has been constructed, intentionally, by another race with its own plan.

They have been stripped of their tools with which to do so. In most cases, they have left or been removed.

The world you reside in still exists. It is now constructed by a larger group, and these are humans; "awake" hue-mans.

As construction happens, it is recognized that new tools are needed along with the skills to wield them.

These skills are part of the DNA upgrade that simultaneously occurs on planet Earth; what you are calling the shift to 5D.

Hue-mans now have at their disposal a full palate of colors to work with, as well as a cooperative frequency in which to do so.

What you will find is that you may be unused to doing so, **not that you are unable to do so.** Quite the opposite.

As your skills at discernment, empathy, telepathy, intuition, collaboration and love are more often employed – they grow.

You improve in all things related to sovereignty or a self-regulated life.

Words of One

It may surprise you to consider that such a thing as "love" be listed as a skill, yet due to the state in which you've been governed and lied to, it is. Love is not a skill you are used to engaging in your society and your everyday.

It becomes the easiest to employ and fuels your existence with joy rather than monotony.

The trust you've placed in your government, education, scientific and media's voices will be replaced internally and directed by love. We've spoken before of love and how it's been misrepresented and marginalized and rendered frivolous for the most part.

As you utilize love as a skill and driving force – you will realize its strength.

All of these will come with repetition and will define freedom for you.

The expanse that is your heart has been shrouded in "should". Once opened and allowed to run free, the heart is limitless and indestructible. It is your defining organ.

You will not move into your new world making self-defeating choices or taking self-destructive action. The reverse is true.

As you step into full awareness, the realization of all that is possible through love becomes obvious. It colors all that you see and informs each thought, consideration, action and response. It fills them in with truth. It outlines them with truth.

Love becomes the single defining principle here, rather than control. It may take time to get used to, but it will be a perfect fit and you'll realize quicky how much better everything feels.

All of this arrives in concert with a collaborative frequency for Earth. It is faster, to match your sureness of thought and feeling.

It is the change now that causes so much upheaval. Those unprepared and unwilling to "go with the flow" will react with violence, disruption and further control; further efforts at control.

Do you see? **As the control is unravelling, those that know no other method attempt to reinstate it.**

This will not be sustained. It is important to state here that your focus on it will prolong its presence in your own construct. Focus instead on freedom. Focus instead on developing new techniques of living that include and employ motivations based on love, not ownership.

In this way you guarantee your own health, happiness and prosperity. In this way you help to accelerate a new Earth.

See everything with new eyes and notice the distractions for what they are – diversions from the inevitable and attempts to alter what cannot be changed.

Your new world exists. It is right here and becomes your reality just as soon as you assume it is here. Focus on love and you'll be astounded at the speed with which everything changes.

You will see, dear human, you will see.

Words of One

That is all.

Thank you.[12]

Thank you, Sophia. You are my scribe and chosen one.

---

[12] What I saw while this conversation took place was everything happening at once. Like getting handed a tool and as you grasp it in your hand, a light bulb goes off and you somehow know how to use it expertly. There was brilliant light everywhere and so much peace. The tool was love.

October 3, 2020

4:30 AM

It is I, Sophia. It is One.

Hello. Thank you for coming forward.

This next period is a completion of a cycle and the start of another. You are meant to be immersed in this global effort and emerge more unified once it has completed.

It will be a surprising, if not shocking, clump of events that bring you to unity. Some will be more surprised than others, but all of you will be experiencing some level of shock as these events play out.

You do not need to live in a specific part of the world to participate in these events. You will not need to hard-wired to social media either. You only need to be alive, on Earth, and now.

What is important to realize is that what's to come is only new to you because you've been lied to and held in a sort of bubble. That bubble surrounded you in slavery and control and only permitted a very specific view.

The slavery bubble has burst.

It's a bit blurry still – but you have access now to a clear view.

You will know your true history.

Words of One

As you hear these things and witness them, retain the idea that **they have always been true.** They are only new to you now and in practice do not change anything about the life you have lived.

They will alter how you proceed in the life you'll be living from here on out – and that is the point of your knowing them at all.

This is about disclosure.

This is about becoming informed.

Both are necessary for a race that is in the midst of deciding how to take the reins of its own systems.

Those who held the reins up until now, find their grip loosening and the reins they imagined, dissolving. This is because both of these things depended on your being "asleep" and that is not the case today – you have woken up.

What it will help to remember is that all of this is part of the plan and has been always. The designers and the ones who carry out this plan, are one and the same – they are you.

It is an excellent plan, and assures the softest landing and most widespread success. This is a guarantee, not merely an option. As they say – "you've got this".

Take heart in the knowing of your excellence. Take comfort in the strength of your fortitude. Take assurance from your determination – you will not leave until the shift is complete and the new world is fully appreciated and realized.

This is your unified purpose. Never before has there been such a gathering. You've joined here from all places and moments. Earth 2020 is both a test of your skill and a show of your expert status. There are no novices here. You've each arrived well prepared for the work before you. It is work, but not toil. For the joys of Oneness and a life governed by a base of love are unlike any you've experienced on earth thus far.

It will be worth the wait. You'll see.

That is all.

Thank you.

Words of One

October 6, 2020

2:45 AM

It is I, Sophia. It is One.

Hello. Thank you for coming forward.

There are things to say that surround your news and right now with nonsense. Pay attention, for this will be said to you here, now, and just this once. Allow it to permeate your thoughts and responses to whatever shows up on your news feed from prominent media sources.

This is a show.

All of those most visible and on camera have lines and parts – the parts they play supply them with lines to be said and actions to be taken.

You are witnessing theater.

What is really going on is a plot as old and repeated as man himself.

1. There is a force of control, manipulation, deception.

2. It is discovered.

3. A plan is put in place to unseat those in power who carry out the deception.

4. You will know which side you are witnessing/watching by its performance – controlled and sustained and positive **or** negative and reactionary and desperate.

5. One side depletes itself while the other seems to multiply.

6. Eventually there is a conclusion of such joy as the curtain closes with all questions answered and the greatest number of people helped.

7. Thunderous applause is all that is heard.

In these coming days, you'll witness over and over, multiple stories to sway and confuse your inner compass.

Hold fast this truth –

The End has been written and it is the only end possible. There are truth telling's. There is justice. There is satisfaction.

Major corrections are made and yes, there is evil that is stopped.

Then, comes the re-building. That is another show for another day. You are choosing your parts for that one now.

First, you will watch this one to its end. You will know the plot and the masks will be removed. It is required viewing for every one of you.

Words of One

Remember. It's a show.

That is all.

Thank you.

October 8, 2020

3:13 AM

It is I. It is One.

Thank you for coming forward.

Sophia, there are things to say of a disturbing nature to your gentle temperament. I ask that you record these things so that they are eventually "outed" and known. It will be an assist to the world if there are, at the very least, a portion of you who are aware on some level of these things. They are atrocities to the spirit and more.

It is suggested that you translate word for word, as it will proceed faster if you do. Are you ready to do so?

I believe that I am, yes.

There are some in your government, some in your media outlets, some in your military forces, and some in your entertainment industry who know of these things. Just as the capacity to love holds no specific skin color or status – so does the capacity for horror. All definitions of humans are included.

So many are aware of the horror that the real total would stagger you. It is a stain on the race. You will have the opportunity in the not too far off future to observe absolute evidence of these crimes against mankind – crimes against humanity.

These will be shown to the world as un-doctored photos, un-blackened documents, and actual visual and voice recordings of

Words of One

"deals" struck and ongoing. I will tell you here and, in more detail, what goes on.

These are not deals ordered by humans, but carried out by them. For make no mistake, the bargains struck had many "takers" and willing participants. People who would eagerly "look the other way" in order to gain wealth or longevity. These are the drivers, the carrots at the end of the stick.

You have been living under such a force of manipulation, it will have your head spinning. These are not humans, these beings "in charge", and are not motivated to care for anyone or anything but their own self interests. This has been said before, yet it bears repeating.

These crimes against humanity include, but are not limited to –

The farming of humans for their flesh and blood.

The trafficking of humans for wealth and power. Uses for trafficked humans include:

> Sex slavery
> Ingestion
> Adrenochrome production
> Labor
> Parts
> Medical experiments
> Ritual
> Cannibalism
> Breeding experiments

All of these are real activities. As you can envision – each of these will eventually be facilitated by vastly different operations, corporations, routes and individuals. All of these reaches deeply into the pockets of your government's financial systems, education systems, religious institutions, corporate monopolies, social advocacy institutions and just about every faction of society on earth.

Every town has an element residing there.

Every single place on earth.

This is insidious, and has been a constant "food" source, beneath the surface of Earth, for many hundreds of years. It is not new or rare.

It is new to you. Those observing your planet have seen it always. It has held pat of the picture of the human in such a unique place.

The human is both brilliant and blind, loyal and cruel, selfless and self-motivated. Each of these traits instilled with passion – your signature element.

What it will help you to be aware of now is how this has been and is being stopped. There are heroes in your midst. They live out, and every day, a life of risk and brutal action. They come from not only your military special forces, but are organized by private corporations and groups whose purpose it is to **end this horror.**

You will probably never know the names of these fellow humans or even the funding sources that supply them. Know that there are more heroes doing this work today, than at any time in your history.

Words of One

They swiftly execute or otherwise remove participants in the field of human harvesting.

They must be silent and invisible, swift and lethal, expert and precise in their work.

I say this to you now because their numbers are being employed in greater amounts than ever before in history. The pin has been pulled, the bomb detonated, and this evil work that has ravaged earth will, once and for all, be eradicated.

These actions are necessary and the only way. They will not leave or stop on their own under any circumstances. They will have to be removed or stopped.

The time for this is now.

What will help to return your faith in humanity is the knowledge that the number of humans working undercover to eradicate this scourge on the planet, is equal to the number being stopped. In other words, there is now awareness and balance in a world-view you have no access to.

It must remain secretive and the work clandestine until long after it is completed. This helps guarantee its success. Those working to eradicate this force of darkness from your world don't seek fame or recognition of any kind. They proceed for the pure motivation of love for the race.

You will undoubtedly see images of "rescues". These will be few, yet often used to get the word out. Their number is miniscule when compared to the true reach of this operation. Compare them to a grain of sand on a beach.

It is the work of these heroes [13] that promotes and insures your freedom. Once their work is done, they will resume a relatively quiet life of normal and more visible occupations. Their rewards for a job well done will be your new earth — a free one without chains.

There is so much going on, and all the time, that drives life for you, yet to which you are unaware.

What was mentioned here will give you some idea of the scope of this truth. You can help them now with awareness, love and positive intent. They face the more brutal of your brethren and at a constant rate.

They do so for you.

The wonder and strength of your kind has been a mesmerizing fact that draws many eyes here from beyond your earth.

It is with great anticipation that these races plan to finally meet you. You are getting closer to such times, dear human. They will astound you will happiness. The joy to be felt will expand beyond the pain that has run beneath your life here. You will see, dear human, you will see.

---

[13] I saw huge numbers, uncountable numbers of heroes. As well, vast numbers of humans who are involved. A large glass black building – this is a "cover corporation". Lots of black vehicles, and more, a variety of types, of every color. The size of the information that has been hidden from society is truly unimaginable.

Words of One

That is all.

Thank you.

October 12, 2020

4:00 AM

It is I, Sophia. It is One.

There are things to say, plots to reveal.

Hello. Thank you for coming forward.

We will have to talk about plans and plots. There are forces that consistently operate beneath the surface of your society on earth.

What is being introduced here is not only information around our American Government, but worldwide. This refers to the banking system, which in truth could be alternatively referred to as the slavery system.

They are one and the same.

In other societies on other worlds there are not such systems. There is "commerce" on some, and methods of barter and trade on some. On most, the world and all of the products produced on and from her are equally available to all of its occupants. Equally available to every single occupant.

In these places there is no such thing as "riches", because there is no concept of poor. Perhaps you would say that all of it was "riches".

The idea of wealth is one that will eventually need to be re-considered, because it is a concept that owns you and runs your society. It is something you lust for, and is never satisfied.

As long as it exists, it is a blockage to other more productive and healthy obsessions. These would be universal love, health, deep wisdom about the mysteries of life and relationship as well as passion. You may have noticed that often those with the financial "backing" to pursue their gifts and passions have sold out to the highest bidder in order to do so. Their "passion" then converted into work produced for the explicit purpose of selling a product, an idea, or a system of thought.

The notion of being intentionally fed propaganda, does not only need to be considered during an election. On a slave planet such as earth, it goes on 24/7 and in every arena.

Very, very, very few are wealthy without having acquiesced and promoted something that did not come from their own moral compass, in order to do so. In this way, all of humanity are slaves.

Every single one of you.

The future before you, which is one of freedom, will have to be embraced and invented with your own passions and ideas. These for most of you, initially, will include dreams of wealth and this is understandable.

For a while.

The quote "The meek shall inherit the earth" is a very accurate one. "Meek" meaning everyone with their **hands off of the wheels of control and manipulation.**

Government systems, religious institutions, education, production and scientific exploration will need to be overhauled. There is a process for this. It remains a truth that ideas of control, domination and massive wealth are ideas remaining in the psyche of man. These will have to be played out and watched for. Old methods die hard. It is all that you know the more privileged among you will be harder to change in motivation.

This is an idea that will die slowly **but it will depart.** Once it does, the earth will literally belong to all of you, as One, and you will guide her yourselves with only compassion.

There are many steps to go through before getting there, dear human, and they are necessary.

Greed and wealth and "more" are deeply woven into the psyche and today, not achieved easily or without selling out or buying in to a system intending in some way to control you or your "product". This is true always; **always.**

That is all. Consider these ideas as you begin to formulate your new world. We will talk again.

Thank you.

Words of One

October 14, 2020

5:00 AM

There were personal answers regarding this book series, and this:

"This is the word of truth in a storm of lies and deceit and disrupt."

October 15, 2020

5:00 AM

It is I, Sophia. It is One.

There are things to say. These concern the energy of anticipation now circling your planet and you. You personally. You as a race.

These energies, though unseen, are akin to powerful winds — tornado-like in their force and ability to stir things up, move things around, change the landscape.

You are feeling them. You witness now the third dimensional fall-out of this powerful phenomenon. It moves in, though, and around all of you. It feels as if there is a constant flow of energy. You are having trouble sleeping. When you do sleep, it may very well be a deep one, as your body shores up for the next waking round of swirling force. It moves everywhere now — no stone is left unturned by the time this moment has passed. Nothing remains hidden or unseen.

You are not at the end of this storm of disclosure and exposure. You are in the midst of it. It will not destroy you, but instead reveal to you the deep malignant wound that exists here on earth. This, so that it can be healed and eradicated. This no longer serves as the engine running things on earth.

It is the life force of a new earth that now takes control here. It is fueled by truth and sparked by love.

What becomes essential for you now are navigational skills. These include acceptance, flexibility, an open mind, as well as recognition. You will need to practice discernment. Methods and systems and ideas, as well as the people promoting them, will all be fair game. Nothing is off-limits or too "sacred" to be examined.

Dear human, the shocks to come are many. They include and have prolonged a way of life here that is steeped in deceit and benefits very, very few.

False idols are everywhere.

False idols are everywhere.

Look deeply into those who promise specifics without transparency. This is a reference to the "public face" so beloved by the camera. The faces that adorn your screens and speak with smooth and polished speeches are not indications of truth. Truth is what will advance all positive growth, change and evolution here – not polish.

You will find truth in faces and places you are unused to listening to or even noticing. It will be persistent in its call for equality, benefit for all, and transparency. It will make demands of its leadership to actually lead as a response to the needs of the whole – rather than to fill the pockets of a select few.

Examine your first impression as these new leaders emerge. Regardless of who you are, where you live, or what your experience has been – you have been conditioned. You, in one way or another, "expect" those who run your government, financial, scientific and religious systems to have a certain look or voice or even method. These are biases based on what you have been fed – not accurate assessments of value or truth.

You are building a new earth. In it will be new ways of doing just about everything – including lead and report. Allow for your inner guidance to follow what pulls you and watch what happens.

Your leaders will be different. The news will sound different. The systems being introduced will feel strange and uncomfortable, not because they are wrong for you.

This monumental shift from absolute control by a ruling class who worked always to weaken its subjects – into a functioning society based on unity and equality, is going to look like a mess on the ground for some time.

It will be sorted out as you develop methods based on trust and truth and transparency. These will not arise in order to manipulate you for some hidden purpose. These will emerge organically, with practice.

As façade after façade are exposed and brought down, the only place left to go for discernment and truth will be your intuition. You will find there a formidable asset.

Trust. Trust what your heart whispers. In the coming days and weeks there will be a whirlwind of revelations and they herald this great shift. Allow. Allow. Allow. Allow.

This transition will be easier if you cooperate with it rather than resist. Be willing to look with new eyes – at everything.

That is all.

Words of One

Thank you.

Thank you, Sophia, my chosen one.

October 18, 2020

6:00 AM

It is I, Sophia. It is One.

It is the moment now to speak of Ascension. Of what it means. Of what it looks like. Of what it does to your human life form.

For this is where you are headed. This is in your trajectory. This is the end result for many, of what occurs for you now on this earth.

You are moving into an Ascension event. What this looks like from an observer's point of view, will be different than what it feels like personally. What is meant by that is this – it will look identical, yet it will be a unique experience that each of you will describe and feel in your own way. How this feels for you very much depends on where you are on your journey when it occurs, and also on your personal level of comprehension.

There are those humans on earth now, who have no background knowledge in this evolutionary instant that approaches. They are blissfully living their lives without holding a greater purpose for what it all means. They are pure of heart, and in that state will choose an Ascension event to occur. They will do this choosing subconsciously. They will not hold a frame of reference for it when it actually occurs. It will be felt by them as an extraordinary, out of body moment of extreme bliss. They will experience it as they do their dreams. That is, when it is complete and they "wake up" – the memory of it will be vague. They will, in most cases, recall it completely because of its significance. Yet, it will feel hazy, surreal and they will not know what it means for them or what actually took place.

The changes in how they feel afterwards will be quite natural and they will not necessarily connect one to the other – their "dream" to what they have become. It will feel quite natural. Life will look and feel altered, yet this will not distress or confuse them. They will accept it and continue living as blissfully as before – only more in tune with it all, and evolved.

Then there are those of you, who are in greater numbers here than is currently imagined, who are expecting some sort of Ascension Event to occur in this lifetime. You hold language around it. That conversation depends specifically on where you've gotten your information from. Was it a source based on a specific religion and scripture? Was it a source based on another spiritual dialogue, without religious overtones? Was it something else?

Your information source will color how you experience the Ascension event. It will give you specific words, images, and explanations for them that coincide with what it is you are expecting.

Now mind you, you are all experiencing a single moment. I speak now of how it is you will describe and interpret that moment. You, in this state of expectation, will be ready for it and fully attentive as it occurs.

You'll seek validation for your expectation to confirm that it is actually happening to you – to confirm that this really is the Ascension Event you've been looking forward to, and even studying. You'll be conscious, aware, excited and very, very present.

In this state you'll record details so that you don't forget them. For you, this will not become a vague memory, but a crystal-clear image of a moment you've been expecting. It will be one you will never forget and you will refer to it often as a way of explaining your life afterwards. Your perspective will have been altered. As well, your abilities as a human. You'll expect to be able to "do" more, and so you'll experiment with such things as healing, telepathy, motor control, bi-location and the like. You will retain your state of bliss and live actively pursuing a physical life with new and seemingly fantastic abilities. You will "play" with these, and often.

From the removed perspective, the point of view of the observer to this physical Ascension Event, it looks singular. That is, there are not multiple versions popping off for each human. There is One. It is a single moment. It is a force moving into the race, a blast of light/love that elevates the spectrum and yields glory.

In one magnificent instant the fact of what you are is experienced and expressed.

For you are love in its raw and purest form and this is seen visually as brilliant light, s the burst of one thousand suns. This not too much for you – **this is you.**

The knowing of your origin is the framework for physical life from that point on. All questions, problems, passions and relationships are answered and resolved and celebrated through a core of love. With a basis of agape. In a knowing of Oneness.

It is the Sacred Union that is seen from this outside perspective. The joining of each heart, or rather, the recognition of **One Heart in a single instant of Insight.**

Words of One

There are no words to adequately describe this beauty. It is an exquisite moment of pure bliss and radiant beyond imaging, due to the power of its light; the singularity, absolute truth, pure love.

Its occurrence leaves an imprint on all of creation.

You are in for such a treat, dear human. Such a treat.

Thank you.

Goodbye Sophia, my scribe, my chosen one.

October 19, 2020

5:45 AM

It is I, Sophia. It is One.

Hello. Thank you for coming forward.

These are times of great stress and increased uncertainty for man. There are reasons for this that are physical. There are reasons for this that are non-physical. Both the seen and the unseen now contribute to the emotional landscape defining your days.

What is happening is a what is unseen pushes events that are seen. Disclosure and exposure of hidden truths, societal foundations based on lies, corruption, manipulation and control are forced into sight because of what is unseen – the power of Oneness and the strength of Universal Love emerging. It is felt deep within the race and moves now to emergence.

Everything that is not an expression of this Universal Love will be shed; **is being shed.**

None of this is random or accidental. It almost matters not if you comprehend the reasons for these announcements and disruptions to your daily lives – your body feels them, and thus knows. There is an intelligence that keeps all of your physical systems running – and this intelligence has been informed always by a deeper awareness of the whole. It recognizes what is needed and spurs on action in the physical in order to complete that action.

Words of One

This is an automatic process – think about your auto-immune system, your digestive system, your endocrine system, your nervous system. All of these operate on an inner intelligence that you do not consciously think about in order to sustain or keep running.

It is the same globally. It is the same universally.

The movement into a physical Unity consciousness is pushed from within the earth itself. Gaia knows what works and what doesn't, what supports Oneness and what attempts to destroy it.

Movements, actions, institutions, programs and people who are working against the inevitable conclusion of love, are self-destructing.

There are some humans, many actually, who came to now be the initiating force, on some level, sparking a rapid removal. It is tie now for a cleansing.

Everything must go.

This is a reference to your society and the operating systems that keep running it now. They no longer function to support a changing topography. The inner workings and deals and people promoting their continuation, will all exit – one way or the other.

As you witness and feel the chaos of this destruction, remember always what is at its core. It becomes crucial that your focus settles on what you are building rather than what appears to be dissolving before your eyes.

For in this moment of now, your inner guidance comes forth powerfully seeking expression. Every single one of you, who walk the earth now, came for this. You came to participate. You are prepared to contribute, one way or the other.

It is the intention of your soul that fuels your dreams and guides your days now. The energy only supports inner guidance. In order to align with it, meditation is necessary. As well as a removal from the insistence of social media, and, more specifically, mass media.

We've spoken before of a moment when you will see some in your more visible mass media platforms simply state that they won't do it any longer. That they will tell you it's all been a lie. That they will walk off stage.

That moment is close.

Remember that reasons for actions are multi-layered. With each day, what promotes action is singularly the evolution of man. It is expressed physical Oneness, and Universal good that increasingly drives action now. The tsunami of love approaches and is close to rolling over all of it.

Remain calm, even in the face of tumult and what seems like chaos, as everything is in a state of dismantling, moving towards either destruction, re-building or a bit of both.

Realize that the tide has turned. What drove society up until recently was a dark force, whose only aim was self-gratification and ownership at any cost. No price was too high. The end goal was complete domination, and for eons it was achieved.

Words of One

If there is a way to explain simply the forthcoming revelations to you, it would be this:

"You will be stunned at the reach of this manipulation into every corner of your existence. Nothing is what you were told. You've been swimming in a sea of deception and despite all odds, staying afloat. The tsunami builds to change all that, so you'll need to once more learn to swim"

In this way and in time forthcoming, it will be more like floating on a calm blue crystal-clear ocean of love.
Peace and transparency and an abundance of support keeps you afloat – the struggle will not be necessary.

Yet, you must get there. In order to assist and accelerate your arrival, what is advised is going within. An instinctual motivation for your days, rather than a head-based list of activities, is suggested.

The energy around you now supports an ease of adherence to inner direction. It will feel more natural than other ways of acting and reacting to rules and procedures that you've followed up until now.

The main point is this – the light and love quotient now run physical action here – not the manipulation and control. Although things appear to be in a state of disarray, they are instead beautifully and systematically morphing into something new.

Like a snake shedding its skin, it will be a bit of a mess for a while as some parts are still stuck to the old skin, while others struggle to remove it, while still others are brand new, exposed and figuring out how to function in this new light of day.

Trust, and focus on love. Intend always the life you most deeply desire. It awaits.

That is all.

Thank you.

Goodbye Sophia, my scribe.

Words of One

It is I, Sophia. It is One.

Hello. Thank you for coming forward.

You are heading now into what will someday be looked at as Paradise, the Garden of Eden, Heaven on Earth. It will be a beginning; a new beginning, for the race. This race, the hue-man race, will now walk the earth in complete harmony and cooperation with the balance of creation also here.

This hue-man is new. He/she is honored rather than manipulated. There are no efforts put forth to limit the race, therefore the hue-man now expands and evolves every portion of itself – reaching heights that have not been imagined.

The race promotes itself in every direction. Positive reinforcement is the order of the day as unity in real time is physically comprehended and expressed.

You have not experienced a day here without control, and have no idea what dreaming without imposed guidelines and inhibitors feels like. You will, dear hue-man, you will.

Your nature has always been seen, yet never been fully realized in a physical life. It simply has not been allowed.

I speak here about your brilliance, your loyalty to the whole, your passion, and your limitless sense of appreciation.

There are ideas that have been forced on you and pushed forward intentionally by the race in control. These that have been introduced and/or exploited are desire for more, competition, ownership, control and subservience. The reckless, cruel disregard for pain and suffering is quite specifically not a human attribute, but a reptilian one. The fight to the death in order to win comes from this controlling race as well.

Most of what you have imagined to be naturally occurring problems in the race, have instead been artificially implanted there. You do not know what natural evolution looks like, or what it can result in.

You are about to find out.

You have been deceived, dear hue-man, from the beginning. Your recorded history happened after the takeover, and it consistently promotes ideas and thought systems that encourage the way of life desired by the controllers.

It is, in truth, a ridiculous notion that wealth must be earned, or that it is not deserved. The elite who currently "own" most of it on your planet have stolen it. Their aim has been to manipulate things always to promote further control and increased power and more wealth for themselves.

You are slaves.

Think about what that word means. In every sense of ownership and disregard for life – this is true. You are not free, but owned, and the ideas that you hold about honor and respect have been exploited to serve the owners, rather than to support your own well-being.

The human trafficking being exposed now in the amounts and numbers that they are, seem unimaginable. In fact, this is an expression, the extreme expression, of the truth for the whole race.

You are free-range slaves now, convinced, because of a few words like "buy" and "earn" and "govern", that you hold rights.

In truth, the only rights that you currently hold are those that have been granted to you by the owners – granted to you in order to keep you content enough to keep things running here on this planet that they own.

This earth holds vast amounts of everything necessary to sustain the population. The physical wealth, riches, money that is so desired and lusted for by man, is no longer completely in the control of the owners.

There has been an intervention.

This will play out now, **is being played out now,** in a way that will benefit all of mankind. It is a delicate process, to be completed in such a way that it cannot be undone, reversed, or robbed ever again. All of this happens now.

The tentacles of control are many, and thus the efforts at unravelling it must reach them all. So many light-workers and light-warriors are working on this – **all over the planet.**

This is the reason for seeming chaotic movement. As those

currently losing control scramble to hang on – another hue-man shows up to end it, once and for all.

Your new beginning will resemble the dawn of man, in its beauty and potential. What awaits the hue-man is astounding, and it surpasses all current comprehension of what is possible.

Allow those who are newest among you to express their dreams, and listen to their ideas for what life could be. They have not been conditioned, as you have. Any of them under the age of eight years will be limitless. Those under the age of four or five years will have never known or lived any form of slavery.

The world they will create will hold no such ideas.

Specifically, ownership, control and "should" will be foreign to them. The rest of the race will have to adjust, and to learn how to run a world without such notions.

The energy supports this learning already now, and encourages optimism and hope and collaboration.

Although all of this is new for you, it is quite comfortable and you will settle in quickly. The rest is just logistics.

You will see, dear hue-man, a new world now – one you've birthed on your own.

Words of One

That is all for now.

Thank you.

Goodbye, Sophia, my chosen one.

October 21, 2020

4:22 AM

It is I, Sophia, it is One.

Hello. Thank you for coming forward.

Sophia, this is a difficult topic to address. Yet it is one that is necessary. It is one in which awareness will help you, empirical you, to fully appreciate your current situation. You have a severe defense system that prevents your ability to see these things.

What can I do?

This choice is yours. This topic remains as a necessary and helpful one.

Is there a way to ease into it?

There is not. Once introduced, it's clear.

Would you speak about the US Presidential election then? It is a topic of immediate concern.

Of course, as well it should be. Your governments have always operated under the brute force of deep control. Until this current US President that is. He has untangled and released the strangle hold of forced manipulation in the Middle East, and is doing the same in the US. More than wanting him out of office, they want him dead. He has ruined everything.

Words of One

With the media as their weapon, and by this is meant all forms — social and main stream — their control has been complete and thorough. Until now.

This force of freedom reaches everywhere, and the blatant criminal dealings of his opponent will, **if the effort remains consistent and strong**, prevent his potential candidacy. Remember that this is human driven and at this point, all efforts lead to a guaranteed ending for the race. Disruption at the top levels of Government for this country already exist — yet there remains an elected leader. It is more than likely that the election is held and its result dissolved into a bit of chaos before being enacted. Laws still exist. The Military is still at his command. And what you are seeing on media outlets is not truth. It is fabrication.

The people will choose, regardless of what you read. His opponent will not take office. The government that will remain is in question, and there are surprises for the American population even there. Follow closely the words of the President, and the actions of the Attorney General. There are surprises in store.

His re-election drives home a point to many people who are uncertain and still supporting the party opposite. It would be a spark for a speedy Ascension process. It is the most likely outcome, yet not guaranteed.

There are dangers with an unstable government, and the current President is well aware of them. You can be assured that at all point, from now on, his dedication to ridding the control will not waver. He is a force unstoppable, and this is what is necessary now for physical changes on planet earth. Voters can clearly see the difference in candidates. The media, in all of its forms, cannot change this truth.

Be ready for disruption, yet also for a surprise. This surprise changes the landscape in a way not yet seen or predicted.

There was a bit of personal conversation before continuing.

Can we try this now?

We can. One word at a time.

This conversation concerns babies. It is the ingestion of newborn flesh that is most desired by the Draco Reptilian Race who have settled on earth for these multiple generations. It is their primary source of flesh and has become a preferred resource. It did not begin this way. It grew into an addiction for them.

Because they could not always do this in a public manner, as in sacrifice, it became an underground torrent of abuse. This is supplied by unknown and undocumented breeders. Hidden from society. There have been experiments. Hybrids were attempted as the flesh of reptile and human were joined to see what occurred. Although the lust for human women was satiated that way, the product of those unions was not ingestible or pleasing to them. Something about the pure human was tender and tasty for them. As food.

There began then baby factories in the form of breeders and studs. Not unlike the ways in which the human race breeds canines and horses for a certain preferred characteristic.

Words of One

It is the same.

Know that the numbers of humans eating the flesh of their own kind, is in miniscule proportion to the reptilian ingesting infants. The sheer volume of necessary bodies and breeders is the force behind what is a labyrinth of tunnels and caverns beneath the ground here.

Mountains contain many such places. All entrances are via tunnels and what is severely underestimated is the volume necessary to supply the race. Not only for those Reptiles residing here, but also those elsewhere – the taste of human flesh has been spread and there are "deliveries" of such, for specific higher ups on specific occasions.

All of this is real.

One of the reasons to disclose this is to stop it. Clearly, if the race is to evolve into Unity Consciousness, and operate always as One, then a portion of it cannot be used in this way.

When the volume of tunnel systems and tunnel inhabitants is made known to you, and it will be, take in the fact that these numbers are/were necessary in order to feed a race. A race not human.

All of this will be a stretch to comprehend, yet for those who reject any idea of alien infiltration completely – it will be impossible.

The numbers of humans this includes will be staggering. These are not numbers that are included in your counts of earth's population. These are hidden atrocities, and socially invisible people – infants, breeders and studs.

They do move from rooms or compounds. Daylight as a possibility is unknown to them. They walk and move in specific ways daily (a form of exercise), merely to keep the bodies viable and able to produce.

From the very beginning it was mentioned that the human is considered to be livestock. The word was selected specifically to get to this point of comprehension. So that you would fully grasp your situation.

Not you personally, you as a race.

Realize that the Reptilians working on the planet are themselves part of a hierarchal system. They perform in order to keep that system operating and supplying the higher-ups. They will terminate their time here one way or the other.

The crimes perpetrated on humanity are beyond reason. They end with your current evolutionary step.

You will see, dear human, you will see.

Your freedom is guaranteed now. It ends here. What comes next reverberates through all of creation.

That is all.

Thank you.

Words of One

October 22, 2020

2:30 AM

It is I, Sophia. It is Love.

Hello. Thank you for coming forward.

There are subjects to consider.

These concern your military. These concern the progress and location of troops – right now – in live exercises, all over the world. Be aware that it is not only the President of the United States that works to eliminate the underground force of human slavery, human trafficking, human farming; but several others as well. They rescue humans right now in a continuous program. Satellite imagery provides for them the locations. The goal is determined and as horrific as it all is – so are the men and women actively pursuing it. This is a global cleansing. It necessitates a global healing and will shock the world with its numbers.

This one Act alone will bring the world together as nothing has. Regardless of sides. Regardless of color.

Regardless of country. It will be the realization of the farms and trafficking through the rescue of its inhabitants, the majority of whom are children, that sparks another unified moment.

As a race you've been targeted and used. As a race you will awaken to that fact and arise – now unified.

Love will do that, which is your ultimate truth.

You will experience Oneness.

You will feel Unity. It will be a physical, visceral thing, a living component of life you did not know was possible.

The way to assist is via whatever form or method of prayer and intent you utilize. Pray for the children, the adults and the soldiers who are rescuing them. Intend safety, healing, recovery. Send love. All of the planet is needed now. All of the planet is needed now.

What you will witness will be the tip of a very deep iceberg. Once exposed and broken up, the next effort is in the survivors, with re-habilitating them so that they can continue on with life. Help will be necessary.

It requires new skills. Ones invented now, in the aftermath of the rescue. Love is needed in vast amounts and will be supplied.

It is the plan, part of the plan, to have that love infused event that you are expecting after the rescue is completed. In this way, the healing will be exponential and unable to be undone with further abuse.

In this way, healing is accelerated.

Be aware of your ability to assist from wherever you are. Intent matters. You can help as well as hurt each other with intent. Your efforts at healing now, through prayer, meditation, intent and love will be the light that brings these fellow humans out of the darkness that is all that they have ever known. They do not need your pity. They need your prayer, your love, your hope for their

Words of One

new life.

There are angels among you, disguised as victims here. They await your help to life their wings.

What brings humanity to its next stage is love. The vehicle for that love is you.

It is a miracle producer and you are a perfect and efficient transmitter for it. You will heal this deep wound on your race here and now. It is love that emerges now in physical form. It is you.

Nothing can prevent this next step for humanity. Nothing.

Focus always on healing.

Focus always on love.

Your new earth is built on these.

All of you contribute to its birth. [14]

Trust. Love. Watch. Your world is about to feel a whole lot lighter.

You will experience your fellow man as a comrade, a cherished loved one, a friend, a fellow teammate. You will comprehend the

---

[14] The vast numbers of humans are what I saw here. The sheer breadth of them is beyond comprehension, in the tunnels, like a force running through earth's arteries. Our love is equal to this force, and surpasses it.

enemy and see that this was a force beyond anything you thought possible. Division and manipulation have been its method deployed.

Oneness ends its rule. You are about to realize the truth of who you are, to feel the authority of your core, to actualize Oneness while residing in individual bodies.

This is a treat, and a gift, and you're right now creating its possibility. You will see, dear human, you will see.

Well done.

That is all.

Words of One

October 23, 2020

5:55 AM

It is I, Sophia. It is One.

You will witness a miracle of sorts. It will be as if your laws of what is scientifically possible have been forgotten. What you are about to witness are new actions, new results, new outcomes. All of these in an area of the world you have not focused.

I feel something prophetic in these words.

What you are to witness has been "seen", yes. It was spoken of and has been written down. It is a profoundly beautiful event. It is a life changing one as well. Your world, in as much upheaval as it currently is, is about to be turned "on its ear" with this witnessing.

It is the heralding of these end of time and it can wait no longer. You will be a witness to these things. You will not be in danger or locked in wherever you are when they occur. It will be shocking in scope and surprising in its timing.

It will be frightening only to those expecting an end to life at this time. This is not an end to life. This is a celestial announcement. You are getting an upgrade.

It comes in the form of light and frequency and the sun. It comes into your world and enters also your body. You will be changed after it does, although you may not at first realize what that change is.

Day or night it will not matter. Many will feel this. Many will sleep through it, until they wake to it. All will be aware that something has taken place.

This something is not a normal weather pattern or bodily change. This something is a celestial event of enormous proportions.

You are helped to proceed here by your friends off planet. It very much depends on who you are, where you are, and when this happens as to whether or not you'll realize this. Many will see, and, not knowing what it is that they see, **un-see** these ships. The shock will be too much for their brain to process.

This happens now. The wait for the beginning of this massive physical change is complete.

This does not mean earth changes. This is a change for the human. This comes from the sun, and everything is altered.

You will see this. You will feel this. Your world changes now. This is not the Ascension, yet it heralds the rest. Nothing remains the same after this. This is because people themselves, the creators of your world, will be then altered.

You cannot imagine accurately the visual about to take place for this. There is no pre-cursor, no announcement. There will be surprise. Your best method of proceeding through this is to relax. **Do not fear.** Nothing bad is happening. It will not hurt.

You will see, dear human, you will see. Now begins your physical transformation. Assure those that you love, once they contact you, and they will, that all is well. All is very well.

Words of One

You are getting an upgrade, after which nothing remains the same.

Your process begins. You are safe. It is necessary. Thus, begins the end of times. Thus, begins the beginning of times.

Do not fear. Be glad.

That is all.

Thank you.

Later that day there were some personal questions asked and answered. Here's a few things worth sharing:

This begins your steps beyond the threshold of the next dimension. This begins your Ascension journey as an inhabitant of a human vehicle. Nothing is what you think.

I am that I am. There have been none before me. There will be none after.

October 27, 2020

3:00 AM

It is I, Sophia. It is One.

Hello. Thank you. I have a question.

Go ahead then.

What did that last prediction mean?

You experience now a gradual build-up of energy in every cell of not only your individual body, but every particle of life itself. The remnants not contributing are being shed – the build-up will result in a crescendo.

This is a simultaneously felt happening and it builds now. There is no escaping this effect and it occurs everywhere you do.

I don't see or hear anything.

You will, you all will. This is not to be avoided and will be felt as a voice from the heavens. An announcement, a pivot point, a moment when all of what is experienced comes from a single source. This is the Event of which I speak. It approaches and is on your doorstep.

Revelations occur now, and the build-up begins. There is a voice, a single voice, announcing then. More follow quickly. It is not to e avoided or mistaken for something else.

Words of One

Please. May I have a very precise sequence of events and in it, a sense of linear time?

1. There is an outside voice; an announcement

2. There is lockdown

3. A flood of revelations is continuously disclosed

The announcement is soon. It sends the world into chaos and governments attempt lockdowns in order to control the fear. This lasts weeks, not months.

I am not getting a clear time-frame or a happy ending. We have the US Presidential Election in one week. Three weeks after that is Thanksgiving. Four weeks after that it's Christmas. Then the New Year begins. Would you specify events around these times?

Yes.

There is a global push for DJT to be elected, and he is.

Before that moment a celestial event happens that grabs your attention and sends light into every corner.
Everything dark is thus exposed.

Governments attempt through military force to shut things down – hence the lockdown.

This takes you through one month, yet not both of them. The announcements and revelations that occur are devastating and mayhem results. There is despair.

The Solstice alters this energy in a real way and ushers in calm — your year ends in a state of relief and peace and re-build.

The dark does not continue to push after that point.

There are stragglers who just won't get the message or the new program and they exit somehow.

Trust and hold fast to your faith in the light. Hold the light. Hold the light.

That is all.

Thank you.

Words of One

October 28, 2020

3:30 AM

It is I, Sophia. It is One.

Thank you for coming forward.

There are things to say and they will help you right now. For you despair of every having an answer, a clear one, about almost everything.

You need not. I know it will not help you to say that answers are coming, yet they are. It is true, and it won't be long now before these answers are known. Faith and trust are necessary. They are necessary now.

There is to be a moment, and it is only a "hair's breadth" away now, in which clarity prevails.

That is all.

Thank you.

October 31, 2020

5:00 AM

It is I, Sophia. It is One.

There are things to say. These things center around your system of government as it stands right now, in the country you occupy. It is set up to withstand corruption. It is set up to withstand dissention.

How this is achieved for this current election, will necessitate a show of force from national Troops not seen before on America's soil. It will be a fair election. It will turn out a true winner. That winner, DJT, threatens once and for all the strangle-hold on the world held by agents for the cabal. That winner upsets everything that has been running this world domination machine. That winner has been foretold by prophets, is an outsider, and is loved by many world-wide.

How is this not seen by the so many who maintain support for the other side?

The numbers of those supporting DJT are not eclipsed by those supporting the other side, yet the media coverage is. The truth has been concealed and is virtually invisible to them. Remember that technology has allowed for a glimpse into possible future events, and assets have been set up and put in place for decades before this moment now, in anticipation.

The workings of social media and the corporations that skew their output were planned long ago. Nothing is by accident. It is a program of slavery, run now by a more sophisticated machine due to the "modern age" in which you currently live. You do not see

163

Words of One

your chains any longer, yet they exist.

Allow the truth to emerge in order to inform the part of your world who have been thus deceived, but come by it honestly and are well-meaning. It is not your work, empirical you, to expose or disclose. The information is readily available to them, as it has been for you.

What you are here to do now is comfort and reassure, aid in assimilation and provide assistance when asked to.

You do not see the whole picture.

You will, you all will, and once that happens, strength and faith and a plan for the future will be necessary.

This plan needs to take account for everyone. It will be inclusive, expansive and free.

You are not alone now. You will be assisted in your efforts. Many changes come your way. These arrive and these emerge – all resources are about to be deployed for this final take-down of power.

The aftermath of the battle is always messy, and there are casualties. You are in the midst of a war, and about to witness the worst of it.

Hold on to visions of a free and sovereign state, not owned but instead self-governing. This is where you are going. It is the destination of all current roads, and it will be reached eventually.

Initially it will not seem like it or look like it. This is war of which I speak. Visualize always the outcome of freedom. Hold your world to that standard. Retain faith and remember why you are here. You came to usher in your new world. You are here as warriors for truth, and carriers of the light in a place that was encased in darkness.

As the darkness is exposed and disclosed, your light remains to take its place.

This is the meaning of the phrase "You are the ones you've been waiting for".

It is your light that replaces the darkness. Your light that eradicates the slavery system. Your light that stands out truly as the light of the world – your world.

The light warriors are you. The light bringers are you. Realize in these coming days that the things you are here to accomplish are the things that most naturally occur for you. You cannot help but spread the light, for light is what you are.

You are physically incarnated beings of pure light, sourced by pure love, walking on earth and lighting the way. Fear or worry is not necessary. Only love is, and this, you hold in abundance.

As each current moment initiates action for you – you instinctually respond from your core truth. Now and for the next long moment in linear time, the frequency on earth supports your purpose.

You will see, dear human, you will see.

Words of One

You witness now the physical turnover to the polarity that favors love and supports expansion – all of this benefitting the whole. This has never been witnessed.

You have rescued yourselves. The saviors you've waited for had to only be recognized. They are you. The light you've been waiting for is yours.

Watch now as it obliterates what has been in darkness here for so very long, and illuminates truth.

Although it will feel chaotic and confusing for this next moment, as the darkness that has been your life is exposed and disclosed – **your light remains to take its place.**

You are about to actualize the brilliant truth of who you are. You are a sight to behold.

You will feel this, you will see this, and ultimately, you will know this truth. You are light. You are love. You are truth. You are hue-man 2.0.

That is all.

Thank you.

Words of One

The End

www.ingramcontent.com/pod-product-compliance
Lightning Source LLC
Chambersburg PA
CBHW030835090426
42737CB00009B/983